5627 82

P9-BZG-685

ALSO BY MICHAEL MEWSHAW

Sympathy for the Devil

Sympathy for the Devil

FOUR DECADES OF FRIENDSHIP WITH
GORE VIDAL

Michael Mewshaw

FARRAR, STRAUS AND GIROUX

NEW YORK

Farrar, Straus and Giroux
18 West 18th Street, New York 10011

Portions of this book previously appeared, in different form, in *Do I Owe You Something?: A Memoir of the Literary Life*, originally published by Louisiana State Press in 2003.

Library of Congress Cataloging-in-Publication Data
Mewshaw, Michael, 1943–
    Sympathy for the devil : four decades of friendship with Gore Vidal / Michael Mewshaw. — First edition.
        pages   cm
    ISBN 978-0-374-28048-2 (hardback) — ISBN 978-0-374-71119-1 (ebook)
    1. Vidal, Gore, 1925–2012—Friends and associates. 2. Mewshaw, Michael, 1943—Friends and associates. 3. Authors, American—20th century—Biography.   I. Title.

PS3543 .I26Z79 2015
818'.5409—dc23
[B]

2014016971

Designed by Jonathan D. Lippincott

Farrar, Straus and Giroux books may be purchased for educational, business, or promotional use. For information on bulk purchases, please contact the Macmillan Corporate and Premium Sales Department at 1-800-221-7945, extension 5442, or write to specialmarkets@macmillan.com.

www.fsgbooks.com
www.twitter.com/fsgbooks • www.facebook.com/fsgbooks

1   3   5   7   9   10   8   6   4   2

For Donald and Luisa Stewart

I spend most of my time in California. I feel I am fueled by rage and by the political climate there. I am angry most of the time when I am there, which might be unbearable for someone else, but for me it's fuel for my writing.

—Gore Vidal, from an interview late in his life

Sympathy for the Devil

Introduction

Despite his aloof and at times forbidding demeanor, Gore Vidal managed to project an image that persuaded millions of people around the world that they knew him on a personal basis. For more than sixty years he remained a bestselling writer, an influential social and political commentator, and an intellectual force whose work had an impact even on those who never read him. The author of judiciously researched historical novels (*Burr*, *1876*, *Lincoln*) as well as outrageous, genre-defying postmodern texts (*Myra Breckinridge*, *Myron*, *Duluth*), he also wrote successful Broadway plays, countless film and television scripts ("countless" because he was frequently and unfairly denied screen credit), and hundreds of book reviews and essays on subjects ranging from sexual identity to religious fundamentalism, academic charlatanism to American imperialism.

Twice he ran for public office on the Democratic ticket—for Congress in 1960 in New York's twenty-ninth district and for the Senate in 1982 in California. Though he lost both times, he was a credible candidate, not another celebrity indulging in a publicity spree. Nothing demonstrated the seriousness of his aspirations more than his willingness to plow hundreds of thousands of dollars of his own money into his campaigns. It's worth noting that in 1960, running alongside John F. Kennedy, Vidal proposed an alternative to the military draft, a national volunteer program that he claimed Kennedy adopted as the Peace Corps.

With his telegenic good looks and urbane manners, Vidal became a fixture on talk shows when TV was in its infancy, and he grew old in the media spotlight, sitting for interviews in a wheelchair well into his eighties. He famously proclaimed that "sex and television are the two things in life one should never turn down," and he regarded every encounter with an audience as an opportunity to deliver lapidary quotations and wicked punch lines. Who can forget his devastating riposte after Norman Mailer took a wild swing at him: "Once again words failed Norman."

He wasn't joking, however—not entirely—when he observed that all the world's problems could be solved if people did exactly as he told them to. A strong didactic streak underpinned his most whimsical humor and audacious fiction. Studded amid the comic riffs of *Myra Breckinridge*, for example, are self-contained mini-lectures on the French *nouveau roman*, environmental pollution, and population control. As he once told an interviewer, "I believe in the usefulness of books. I am not much interested in art for art's sake."

A contradictory as well as a controversial figure, Vidal insisted, "I am never my own subject." He repeated this mantra, ignoring the fact that he had for decades been retelling his life story—or what purported to be an accurate personal narrative—piecemeal in his essays. For a man who professed to abhor violations of his privacy, he somehow produced two volumes of memoirs, *Palimpsest* and *Point to Point Navigation*, plus the lengthy captions for a photographic hagiography, *Snapshots in History's Glare*. He also cooperated with two authorized biographers.

Tales about Vidal's childhood—each shard of the mosaic set in place by the author himself—infiltrated almost every article about him. His mother, Nina, was a shrill social climber and manipulative alcoholic perpetually on the prowl for rich men. His father, Eugene, had been a football star at West Point and competed in the pentathlon at the 1920 Olympics. Subsequently, he became the national director of aeronautics during the Roosevelt administration. Then he switched to the private sector as an executive at several airlines that were the precursors of today's aviation conglomerates.

When Vidal's parents divorced, he and his mother moved in with her father, Senator Thomas P. Gore of Oklahoma, and his deeply conservative southern wife. The senator was blind, and Vidal grew up reading aloud to him. He nostalgically recalled leading his beloved Dah by the hand onto the Senate floor, and he claimed that he sometimes sauntered into the Capitol barefoot, a dead ringer for Tom Sawyer.

After Nina married Hugh D. Auchincloss, an heir to the Standard Oil fortune, she and Gore took up residence at Merrywood, a baronial mansion in McLean, Virginia, just outside Washington, D.C. Vidal remembered the house as anything but merry, and the couple eventually divorced. As Gore was at pains to point out for the rest of his life, Jacqueline and Lee Bouvier soon supplanted him as Auchincloss's stepchildren. Gore's bedroom became Jackie's, then Jackie and John F. Kennedy's during visits after their marriage. Vidal puckishly remarked that sleeping there carried a curse.

Vulnerable to accusations of name-dropping, Gore might have defended himself, as Martin Amis has, by maintaining that given the prominence of his family, it could hardly have been otherwise. Unwittingly, he became a name-dropper the first time he cried out "Dad," "Bommy," and "Dah."

For much of his youth, Vidal was stashed in a series of boarding schools, each chosen, he believed, to keep him out of his mother's meticulously groomed hair. Ever on the hunt for another wealthy husband, she had a succession of lovers, including Clark Gable, and showed little interest in her bookish son.

With the outbreak of World War II, Vidal joined the army right after graduating from Phillips Exeter Academy. Despite his family's political connections and his father's ties to West Point, he wound up as an enlisted man, not an officer, serving in the Aleutian Islands off the coast of Alaska as the first mate on a freight supply ship. The experience provided the setting and plot of his first novel, *Williwaw*. Published when he was still in uniform and barely out of his teens, it became a bestseller and provided him with the money to live independently from his family.

Vidal's early years might have supplied the raw material for the kind of now-popular memoir about family dysfunction. All the basic building blocks lay close at hand—childhood rejection bordering on outright cruelty, rampant alcoholism, parental promiscuity. Gore had only to choose whether to portray himself as a self-made man triumphing over adversity or as a sad, wounded figure isolated at the top rung of the ladder to success.

He did neither. It wasn't in his nature to snivel or complain—not in public, at any rate—and it wasn't his style to display anything except chilly aplomb in the face of disappointment. Whenever he recounted incidents from his past, he did so with a mandarin detachment, portraying his father and grandfather with affection and his mother as a laughable monster to rival the dragon ladies in Tennessee Williams's plays.

As he advanced onto the world's stage, he adopted an air of aristocratic self-possession. Acknowledging no doubt, no insecurity, never any shame or guilt, he appeared to view everyone and everything with gimlet-eyed imperturbability. American political power brokers from both parties, the British royal family, Hollywood royalty, rulers abroad, all his literary rivals—none of them, in his telling, intimidated him. He implied that he had access to all their secrets, especially their sexual proclivities.

When Gore Vidal died in 2012, the stock footage of his life, many frames of it lifted intact from his own writing, got recycled in obituaries and eulogies. Canned anecdotes, polished quips, lordly pronouncements, and great arias of misinformation set off echoes far too deafening to permit countervailing voices. But now perhaps the din that he drummed up around himself has quieted down sufficiently to allow for an alternative assessment of the man.

As someone who knew him for thirty-seven years, I should start by stressing that Gore Vidal was a sophisticated role player and a well-rehearsed performer. He didn't simply write for the stage and the screen; he acted in plays, movies, and TV sitcoms, and he narrated documentaries that kept him in front of a camera for hours at a stretch. Experience and practice taught him that the first character any successful writer must create is himself, and while he often mocked Ronald Reagan, Gore was acutely aware that like the Great Communicator he was a movie star manqué who had to learn by hard graft how to hit his mark and recite his lines.

He once joked to me that he meant to call his first memoir *An Actor Prepares*, cadging the title from Stanislavski. Instead, he called it *Palimpsest*, "a word that no one will know," he said. "But then it's a life nobody will know, particularly after reading the book."

He always pronounced "memoir" as "me-more" because, he reasoned, "it's more about me." But in fact his memoirs contained strikingly little introspection, few truly intimate revelations, and almost nothing about the people he mixed with on a daily basis. He focused—and his authorized biographer docilely followed suit—on boldfaced names and dubious accounts of public events.

There was little in Vidal's me-mores or in his obituaries to suggest that he was generous, hospitable, loyal to friends, and a quiet contributor to charities that benefited other authors. He airbrushed out of the picture almost everything that might have presented him in a conventionally favorable light. He went so far as to deny he had ever loved anyone or had consciously given pleasure to his hundreds of sexual partners. He swore he had never courted favor, literary or otherwise, and never offered or accepted help. Whenever he was confronted with evidence to the contrary, he brushed it off with a withering wisecrack.

There is, I suppose, a school of thought that a writer should be granted after death the wishes he expressed in life. Perhaps Gore Vidal should be permitted to rest in his grave, confident that neither I nor anyone else will reveal what he was actually like. But in the case of a writer whose work and character have so often been misrepresented, I'm convinced that there needs to be a corrective portrait.

That Vidal bears some of the blame for his misrepresentation is undeniable. Nor was the man behind the carefully contrived mask always admirable. While he preferred to pass himself off as a stoic, à la Marcus Aurelius, or a philosophical contemplative, like Michel de Montaigne, he was frequently quite the opposite—irascible, brusque, angry, depressed to the point of suicidal ideation.

Alcohol, massive amounts of it consumed over decades, did him incalculable damage, ravaging his physical and psychological equilibrium. This, it might be argued, was his private business. But because drinking undermined his work and his public persona, I believe that this topic and his long-standing depression deserve discussion.

Although I have no intention of producing what Joyce Carol Oates has described as a "pathography"—the kind of lurid postmortem that dwells on an author's deterioration—I do mean to present Gore as I saw him, and my emphasis and guiding principle will be on what I know, as lawyers say, of my own knowledge. Ultimately, my reason for writing about him arises out of a desire, as Shirley Hazzard put it in *Greene on Capri*, her book about Graham Greene, to show "what it was to be habitually in his company, to walk with him in a street, to exchange opinions, literature, laughter, and something of one's self; to observe his moods and responses, suffer his temper, and witness his attachments; to see him grow old."

Part I

Part I

ONE

The air was hot and sodden with humidity, and although it was October, a summer thunderstorm felt imminent. We caught a bus crammed with commuters and careened downhill to Trastevere through the evening rush hour—one of the four traffic jams that Roman drivers endure each day. Cars stalled us on Ponte Garibaldi. I didn't mind. The bridge offered mesmeric views of the Tiber and of the dome of St. Peter's, gleaming like a bishop's miter off to our left.

The delay also gave me a chance to collect myself and calm my wife, Linda. We were about to meet Gore Vidal, renowned for his acerbic wit and cutting remarks about those who didn't measure up to his exacting standards. Having watched him on television mete out discipline to the likes of William F. Buckley and Norman Mailer, I preferred not to imagine the mincemeat he might make of an American couple in Rome for a year with their six-month-old son.

A mutual friend had passed along Vidal's number and urged me to call him. Over a staticky phone line I recognized the frosty patrician voice that had launched a thousand insults and sparked countless literary feuds. Vidal didn't so much invite us as summon us to his apartment for drinks.

We jumped off the bus at Largo Argentina, a fenced-in square of excavated ruins; fluted columns and cypress and pine trees sprouted from brick rubble. It was one of those precincts of Rome where some ancient buried secret appeared to have burst through the surface of the modern city for the purpose of reminding people that there is no end to the history, no easy explanation of the mystery, of the place. And no explanation of its citizens either. Dozens of old black-shawled crones had arrived for the evening shift, bearing bowls of pasta to feed the mangy cats skulking through the ruins. The resemblance of these women to priestesses propitiating deities made me think we would have been wise to bring Vidal a gift.

At the corner of Corso Vittorio Emanuele and Via di Torre Argentina, the gray-and-mustard-colored Palazzo Origo, shabby despite its august name, had shops on the ground floor, including one of the largest bookstores in the city, a branch of the Feltrinelli chain. On higher floors, the palazzo housed offices, a language school, and private apartments. Gore Vidal occupied the penthouse. When I pressed the intercom at the building's entrance, a crackling voice told us to take the elevator "all the way to the top." But the elevator, a cage about as big as the holding pen in a county jail, wasn't functioning, and Linda and I had to climb flights of stairs whose grimy iron railings and scalloped steps called to mind a Piranesi prison sketch. The hall smelled of garbage and cooking oil, and behind one door a man was shrieking. Perhaps he had been driven mad by the babble of televisions.

Vidal called out to us that kids from the language school must have vandalized the elevator again. At least the screaming madman was locked up today. He said he sometimes had to whip the poor fellow back into his apartment with a dog leash.

On the sixth and final floor—*l'ultimo piano*, as Italians call it—we entered a high-ceilinged *salone* where a fluffy Australian terrier leaped from an armchair and yapped at our heels as we advanced onto a terrace that looked to be the size of a tennis court. While we paused to catch our breath, Vidal asked what we wanted to drink, then shouted for a servant to bring two scotch and sodas.

Sipping a glass of white wine, he identified a couple of the church domes that bubbled above Rome's skyline.

"That's Sant'Andrea della Valle," he said, "the setting for *Tosca*, act 1. And there's St. Ivo, with the corkscrew lantern on top."

Flocks of starlings wheeled overhead—circumflexes of black beating against storm clouds. A gusty wind harped through potted palms and a vine-laced trellis. Vidal stepped over to the terrace railing, and Linda and I followed him and glanced down at Largo Argentina. Cars and buses swerved around the ruined temples like scavengers scuttling past meatless bones. The racket of their horns and squealing tires was deafening; a haze of exhaust fumes stung my eyes and throat.

Undeterred by the noise and pollution, Vidal instructed us—he was, I would learn, a relentless lecturer—that Largo Argentina had been one of Mussolini's extravagant urban renewal projects. In a devious effort to demonstrate that fascism had recaptured the grandeur of the classical city, Il Duce had had marble slabs dragged from other archaeological sites and deposited here for dramatic effect.

In profile, Vidal's face might have been a cameo carved on an ancient medallion—high forehead, aquiline nose, and slightly swollen, slightly insolent mouth. A bit under six feet tall, he had an upright, almost military bearing and wore a blue blazer and gray gabardine trousers, an outfit I would see him in so often I came to regard it as his uniform. At the age of fifty—he had celebrated this milestone on October 3, 1975—his midsection had given in to gravity and showed a bit of loose flesh. Despite a reputation for vanity, he was self-deprecating about his appearance and joked that he used to be the handsomest man in Rome. "Now I'm just another ruin."

When it started to rain, we returned to the *salone*, a hodgepodge of styles and eras, personal memorabilia and motifs. Gilt-framed mirrors reflected an antique marble bust, a stone lion, Indian wood carvings, an Aubusson tapestry picturing three Dutchmen slaying a wolf, and photographs of Princess Margaret, Jack and Jacqueline Kennedy, and Tennessee Williams. A polite visitor might have regarded the decor as a display of one man's eclectic tastes. A connoisseur might have judged that the collector couldn't make up his mind.

At a sideboard, Vidal poured himself a refill of white wine, and as a Sri Lankan houseboy served Linda and me our scotch, Gore delivered a discourse on drinking. No amount of wine, he swore, was as bad for you as hard liquor. "That's the killer—hard stuff." This pronunciamento was followed by one about sex. "Think how many American men kill themselves with two or three highballs before dinner, then wine with a heavy meal. Then they jump right into bed and have sex. My father had a heart attack in middle age. It didn't kill him, but he was never the same again. The trick is to arrange for sex in the afternoon and save the booze and food for afterward."

As the storm intensified, the terrace shutters banged back and forth. Gore didn't bother to close them. "That's it," he said with finality. "Summer's over."

He settled into an armchair, the dog nestled next to him, and Vidal caressed his high-strung pet. The scene seemed out of sync. He had, after all, famously remarked, "I am exactly as I appear. Beneath my cold exterior, once you break the ice, you find ice water." Yet here Gore was sweet-talking a nervous dog named Rat.

A short, stocky, freckle-faced man dashed into the *salone* and slammed the doors against the rain. "I don't guess it occurred to you," he said bristling at Gore. "Where's hashish?"

My first thought was that he meant to roll a joint. But when Gore said, "He's in the kitchen," I realized they were talking about the houseboy. For decades, the help chez Vidal changed on a regular basis but was always referred to as Hashish or LBP, short for

Little Brown Person. With not the slightest nod to political correctness, Gore salted his conversation with references to nig-nogs, fags, and kikes. It wasn't just that he was a product of his era and upbringing; he seemed to delight in saying the unsayable.

He introduced Howard Austen, his companion of twenty years. Like Gore, Howard wore a blue blazer, but with blue jeans faded at the knees. Ginger-haired and fizzing with energy, he had about him the grit and spunk of New York City, the kind of cockiness that served notice that you'd better take him on his own terms or not at all. In his mid-forties, he still came across as a scrappy street kid, undaunted by Vidal's Olympian aplomb. "What the hell?" he said. "Do you know you have a hole in your shoe?"

Gore examined his sole. "Well, it was good enough for Adlai Stevenson."

Howard muttered that Gore just didn't give a damn—a lament I would hear him repeat many times over the years. While he fixed himself a drink, a skinny, bedraggled woman arrived shaking a soaked umbrella. Dowdy, ill-fitting clothes added to the impression of a lady down on her luck. But Gore said Dorothy James was in Italy working on an Al Pacino film, *Bobby Deerfield*.

"A bit part," she demurred. "If it wasn't for Gore, I'd never have gotten it. I've had health problems, and he helped with my doctor bills."

He waved off her gratitude with an indolent whisk of the hand. Though not immune to compliments about his books, he had no interest in gratitude or praise for his charity.

"Don't listen to her. Dorothy was in *Brigadoon* and *Kismet*."

"Not that you'd know that from the credits."

Gore shrugged and delivered a signature line, borrowed from Oscar Wilde: "No good deed goes long unpunished."

While Dorothy James, Linda, and Howard fell into conversation, Gore asked me what we were doing in Rome, and when I said I was on sabbatical from the University of Texas, based at the

American Academy, he mentioned that he had researched his novel *Julian* in the academy library. This led to a discussion of his work habits. "I write in the morning at a table, longhand on yellow legal pads, just like Nixon, when I'm doing fiction. Typewritten when I'm working on an essay or film script."

He stayed at it three or four hours a day, he stressed, and never let houseguests or his social life disrupt his schedule. It nettled him that he had a reputation as a writer who went to too many parties, wasted too much time in Hollywood, and hobnobbed with too many celebrities. In a career of more than thirty years, he had produced a dozen novels, five plays, several collections of essays, and a series of mysteries under the pseudonym Edgar Box. His historical novels, in particular, were time-consuming enterprises dependent upon years of research, all of which he did himself. He wasn't one of those wealthy bestselling authors, he wanted me to know, who hired legions of assistants to do his donkey work.

"Before I start a new novel," he said, "I go into training. I check into a spa, give up alcohol, and fast for a few days to clear my head. I'm no romantic. To write what I do, I have to be able to think. If you know anything about literary history, you know Henry James and Edith Wharton led far more active social lives than I do, and it never harmed their writing." Then, perhaps to tweak my nose, he joked that a steady diet of dinner parties couldn't possibly dry up one's juices as quickly as teaching creative writing.

It was nearly nine by the time the rain stopped and Vidal suggested we go out to eat. He knew a neighborhood trattoria that had a wood-fired oven and "the best pizza in Rome. The kind with thin crust and not too much cheese."

I hadn't expected this. In retrospect, I don't know what I had expected, but certainly not an invitation to dinner. In a curious fashion, despite his princely bearing, he struck me as slightly melancholic, eager for company, reluctant to have the evening end.

Opposite the entrance to his building, there was a snack bar, Delfino's. "Don't worry," Howard said. "We're not going to that dump."

"I go there for the homemade potato chips," Gore said.

"Admit it. You go there for the American college boys," Howard corrected him.

As we strolled through the warren of streets between Largo Argentina and the Pantheon, the cobblestones, lit by shopwindows, gleamed like the scales of a carp, and Gore provided nonstop commentary. On Via dell'Arco della Ciambella, the remains of the Baths of Agrippa were tufted with weeds and wildflowers, and the semicircle of the ruins, he pointed out, suggested half a donut, accounting for the street's name.

The stores on Via dei Cestari called to mind the designer boutiques on Via Condotti, but instead of Gucci shoes, Valentino gowns, and Bulgari jewelry these shops specialized in religious haberdashery. Mannequins decked out as priests and nuns modeled cassocks, wimples, and sensible canonical underwear.

In Piazza della Minerva a marble ensemble erupted from the pavement, as skewed as a dream from the deep subconscious. Atop a pedestal there perched an elephant that bore on its back an upright Egyptian obelisk. "Bernini," Vidal identified the sculptor.

An indifferent prep-school student, he never attended college, yet had made himself into a polymath who assumed that everybody shared his earnestness about knowledge of all sorts. He also assumed people would appreciate his correcting their grammar—"It's different *from*, not different *than*"—and their pronunciation. "It's *flacksid* with a hard *c*, not *flas-sid*," he admonished me.

At the pizzeria, he declared, "The best Italian food is simple. Anytime they get fancy or try something foreign, they foul it up. Rome is the only city in the world where a Chinese restaurant opens one week with great fanfare and by the second week it's serving *bucatini all'amatriciana*."

"You can't blame them for liking their own food," Howard said. "No place in the world can you get pasta as good as in Italy."

"It's the local ingredients," Vidal agreed, "and the water that gives things a distinctive taste."

This was one subject on which he voiced no sarcasm. His love of food was unironic and abiding. But he had to watch his weight and that night he ordered only a salad and a plain pizza margherita. In a matter of minutes, however, he was swiping fistfuls of French fries from Linda's plate. Howard chided him, "Jesus, Gore, you're such a glutton. Next thing you'll be stealing leftovers off other tables."

Gore ignored him and asked me about our mutual friend, who had been diagnosed with multiple sclerosis. He was eager to learn the symptoms of the disease, its prognosis and etiology. "I take my hypochondria *very* seriously," he said.

Although he did most of the talking, he wasn't averse to being interrupted and didn't dismiss opposing views with the kind of peremptoriness that his TV persona might leave one to fear. He was also far funnier and more irreverent than on the Carson or Cavett shows. His conversation crackled with punch lines. Of the French novelist Françoise Sagan, he said, "She's a magnum of pure ether." Then, as if to prove he was no chauvinist who favored American writers, he asked, "What are the three saddest words in the English language?" After a beat he answered, "Joyce Carol Oates."

We discussed American authors who had lived in and written about Italy, and while we both agreed that Henry James was the best of the lot, he also spoke admiringly about a man I hadn't heard of—John Horne Burns—and a novel I hadn't then read, *The Gallery*. Although Burns had blasted *The City and the Pillar* as "a dismal failure" and disparaged Vidal as "our principal rival in the welterweight division," Gore bore him no ill will and told me Burns had been "hounded to death by fag-baiters at the age of thirty-six." In print he had praised Burns's "extraordinary intuition and brains [and] a compassion which has been unequaled by his dry, careful contemporaries who commit as little as possible both emotionally and artistically."

This wasn't, however, to say that he personally approved of Burns, who had, in his opinion, hastened his demise by heavy drinking. It was another object lesson, Gore explained, of the dangers of alcohol. In an interview with Martin Amis in *The Sunday Telegraph*, he had gone so far as to claim that he left the United States "because I didn't want to become an alcoholic, basically. They are all there, for some reason. Fitzgerald, Hemingway, and Faulkner are the classic examples, but it didn't stop with them." His reiteration of this theme prompted a suspicion that I was listening to a man who maybe protested too much.

Vidal was named after his father, Eugene, the celebrated sportsman who had returned to West Point to coach the football team. There appeared to be something deeply Oedipal about a sensitive, unathletic son forsaking his jock-strapping father's name and adopting the surname of his grandfather. But when I asked about this, Gore said that he had simply wanted to ease out from under the double burden of being known as Gene and Junior. He swore he loved his father. His mother was another matter.

He added that at Exeter, where he first began calling himself Gore, he already harbored serious political aspirations. His schoolmates voted him the "class politician," referred to him as Senator Vidal, and predicted he would end up as president—even though they also voted him the "class hypocrite." "I thought that Gore Vidal would look good on political posters," he told me. "And I hoped people who thought well of T. P. Gore would support me."

"It's enough," Howard said, "that your name looks good on books. Who'd want to be president of our fucked-up country?"

It had been only six months since the last helicopter lifted off the rooftop of the U.S. embassy in Saigon, and our talk inevitably turned to post-Nixon, post–Vietnam War America. Corruption and greed, Gore summed things up, controlled the nation, top to bottom. "In the end it always comes down to money."

I didn't disagree, but there was something about the certitude of his sweeping assertion that ignited in me a contradictory spark. I asked if he ever felt guilty about his own wealth.

Where a different man might have reacted angrily to such a question from a stranger, Gore gave it a moment's thought, then coolly replied, "Why should I? I've never exploited anyone. I give fair value for what I get."

But when he received million-dollar book advances, didn't that leave less for everybody else? Wasn't the publishing business, of which he was a major beneficiary, part of the skewed system he decried?

"Well, there's no such thing as unilateral socialism," he said. "I work within the system we have. And as Bertrand Russell put it, I'm a socialist, not a saint. I guess I was born with certain advantages. But I wasn't raised in a bell jar; I wasn't pampered. I've supported myself—and others—since I was seventeen. I didn't inherit my money, as some people believe. Everything I have, I earned."

When the bill came, he wouldn't hear of letting me or anybody else pay a share. "That's how I know I'm not rich. I pick up bills. Rich people never pay. No matter how much money they have, they let other people pay. That's why they're rich."

Walking back toward Largo Argentina, I wondered whether I had spoken out of turn. As I went over in my mind what I had said, I wondered why I hadn't had the good sense to keep quiet. I wondered whether we would ever see Gore Vidal again.

TWO

Years would pass before Gore let me pick up a dinner tab, but it was just a matter of days before I bumped into him again. Rome's expat community, especially its clutch of writers, artists, and film-makers, was small, and we constantly crossed paths in piazzas and trattorias. In contrast to the elbows-out competitiveness I had experienced in academic life, there was an easygoing camaraderie here, and Vidal set an egalitarian tone that carried over to the parties he attended as well as to the ones he hosted. Whether in a group of impecunious journalists or broken-down actors who had been beached after the collapse of Hollywood on the Tiber, he never stood on ceremony, never exhibited the high-handedness he was often accused of.

At his own parties, priests (yes, Catholic priests!), diplomats (mostly from Eastern-bloc nations, none that year from the American legation except for a CIA agent), classical scholars, young sailors, Italian translators, and clothing designers crowded into the apartment overlooking Largo Argentina and rubbed elbows and sometimes other body parts with the occasional visiting movie star or literary eminence from the States.

In effect, we were all there paying homage to Gore Vidal and at the same time collectively celebrating *ottobrata romana*, which extended well into November. On days when a sirocco blew out of North Africa, the air was heavy with heat and sand sizzling with static electricity. On backstreets, women watered down the dusty cobblestones and draped carpets over windowsills and walloped away the grit of the Sahara. Autumn leaves didn't display the same vivid colors as American elms and maples. Still, Rome flamed in radiant shades of orange, red, and purple that rivaled any New England forest. These hues flickered on the city's stones, not its trees. Marble ruins and the baroque facades of splendid palazzi and basilicas captured light that changed by the hour, the play of shadows rippling over convoluted spaces beneath a sky that each evening shimmered like the *vino bianco* that Vidal favored.

Gore and Howard had friends in Rome who remained loyal to them for the rest of their lives. Eventually, they became my friends, too, and when I later moved to Rome more or less permanently, they provided good company and good counsel about the protocols of a country that can be impenetrable to a foreigner.

Donald Stewart had met Gore in the States in the early 1950s, and when he and his Italian wife, Luisa, settled in Rome in the 1960s, the friendship deepened. Though he seldom mentioned it, much less boasted about it, Donald had an illustrious literary pedigree. His father, Donald Ogden Stewart, the model for Bill Gorton in Hemingway's *The Sun Also Rises*, had been a famous humorist and playwright in the 1920s and 1930s. A member of the Round Table at the Algonquin Hotel and one of the best-paid screenwriters in Hollywood, he won an Academy Award for the screenplay of *The Philadelphia Story*.

Donald junior had contributed stories, poems, and Talk of the Town pieces to *The New Yorker* and published a novel in his twenties. After the move to Rome, he switched to an executive position at Playboy International, where he enjoyed a lavish expense account, courtesy of what he called "the Bunny." As generous as Gore when it came to grabbing restaurant checks, Donald acted as a go-between for European-based authors, including Gore, eager to wangle lucrative assignments from Hugh Hefner.

Gore and Howard referred to the Stewarts as "the most beautiful couple in Rome." Donald resembled their good friend Paul Newman, same blue eyes, same handsome features. But he was much bigger, a muscular man, six two and more than two hundred pounds. Where he was blond and amiable, Luisa was a dark, intense former fashion model. In her forties at the time, she remained slim and elegant, with enviable cheekbones and a year-round tan from sailing off the Monte Argentario and skiing in the Dolomites. Every bit as feisty as Howard, Luisa spoke her mind to Gore, and whether she was expressing affection, which made him visibly uncomfortable, or calling him to account for his peccadilloes, she was one of the few people who could bring him up short.

Mickey Knox, another notable fixture in Rome, was as combative and opinionated as Luisa Stewart, but he served more as a court jester and louche drinking companion than someone likely to encourage Gore to toe the line. Depending on which story you chose to believe, Mickey had been either blacklisted as an actor during the 1950s for his leftist sympathies or chased out of Hollywood for seducing a powerful producer's wife. Born and raised in Brooklyn, coarse in vocabulary and conduct, he supported himself as a dialogue coach, a script translator, a film dubber, and a general Mr. Fix-It for movie people who passed through town. In his most impressive credit, he wrote the dialogue for the English version of Sergio Leone's *The Good, the Bad, and the Ugly*. When not dining out on that, he liked to entertain friends with tricks of ventriloquism, pretending to smack restaurant waiters in the face and tear hundred-thousand-lira bills in half.

Mickey clung tenaciously to a rent-controlled duplex apartment near the Spanish Steps. The owner spent decades and thousands of dollars trying to evict him, but Mickey pulled down his helmet and refused to budge. Meanwhile, he turned a tidy profit by subletting the apartment to visiting actors who, as a bonus, received bowls of Mickey's chili—a bizarre concoction lacking meat or beans—which he ladled up at parties he threw for Stacy Keach, Ben Gazzara, Bo Derek, George Segal, Elliott Gould, and various Italian and American directors.

Some of the stars expected more than ersatz Mexican food. Burt Lancaster was one of Mickey's most demanding tenants and insisted on being set up with women. "It'd be different if he was willing to pay," Mickey lamented. "But he thinks he's still box office and that girls'll go down on him for free. You have any idea how hard it is to get Burt Lancaster blown every night of the week? One time when the chick was late, he complained he was having a migraine from the tension and told me to do it. Me, the world's Number One Hundred Percent Heterosexual."

Mickey also knew an enormous number of writers, and over the years he introduced me to Joseph Heller, Pete Hamill, Leo Rosten, Edward Hoagland, Bruce Jay Friedman, and Norman Mailer. Because Vidal and Mailer were feuding during the 1970s, Knox had to exercise uncharacteristic tact and keep them in their respective corners. The role of peacemaker didn't come naturally to him, however. At Gigi Fazzi's restaurant he once heaved a salad at William Murray, a staff writer for *The New Yorker*, prompting a memorable line from Donald Stewart, who had ended up with a lapful of lettuce. "Waiter, there's a salad in my fly."

Mickey eventually managed to orchestrate a reconciliation between Vidal and Mailer, and maybe it was gratitude for such favors that allowed Gore to forgive him his lapses in decorum. Then again, Gore seemed genuinely amused by Mickey's antics.

At a cocktail party for Susan Sarandon, Mickey whispered to me, "Watch this. Here's a line that never fails." Sidling over to Sarandon, he announced, "I'd love to eat your pussy."

She screamed and ran off to complain to Gore. But if she expected him to exile Mickey, she was mistaken. Gore tut-tutted in sympathy and let the matter subside into the vast reservoir of anecdotes about the man whom Gay Talese referred to as the Mayor of Rome and Quentin Tarantino immortalized in his script for *Natural Born Killers* by naming the psychopathic central character after him.

Whenever I read about Gore's relationships with Princess Margaret, Judy Montagu, Lally Weymouth, or members of Italy's Black Nobility, I remember Mickey Knox. I remember his tolerance for all types and his preference for people with distinctive personalities, not necessarily with social distinction. Howard Austen was one such example. Gore's toxic mother dismissed him as "a pimple-faced Jew," but Gore stayed committed to him for life.

Robert Katz was another Jew and, like Howard and Mickey, a New Yorker whose braying voice hadn't softened despite decades of practicing Italian sibilants. Bespectacled and rabbinically bearded, Katz wrote books on topics ranging from Giordano Bruno to the Nazis' occupation of Rome and their murder of hundreds of men at the Ardeatine Caves in reprisal for an attack by Italian partisans. Katz's account of this outrage prompted a libel suit by Pope Pius XII's relatives. The verdict went against him, and if it weren't bad enough to lose a legal judgment to a dead pontiff, Bob was knocked flat near the Vatican by a muzzled dog and somehow bitten through wire mesh.

This wasn't the worst of his misfortunes. Katz sported on the crown of his head a henna-dyed toupee that might have been a yarmulke plastered to his scalp. When Rat, Gore's beloved terrier, suffered a malignant tumor of the mouth, Gore asked me, "Do you know how Rat caught cancer?"

I confessed that I didn't.

"Bob Katz's toupee jumped off and raped him."

Despite the cruel joke, Gore stayed on convivial terms with Robert Katz, just as he did with dozens of Roman acquaintances. Some he kept around because they entertained him. Some he felt sorry for. A few might actually have interested him. I liked to think that I fell into that category. But then I found out that behind my back he referred to me as Youngblood Hawke, the lumbering protagonist of Herman Wouk's roman à clef about Thomas Wolfe.

While that forced me to wonder why Gore was so welcoming, I never had the slightest suspicion that he harbored sexual designs. Not that this possibility didn't cross other people's minds. Some couldn't conceive of a friendship between a straight man and a gay man. Or, because Gore hated the term "gay," between a straight man and a bisexual. At a literary conference, a number of prominent biographers asked why Gore had been friends with me. Did he fancy me? Did he ever make a sexual advance? Did he believe I was somebody he could coax out of the closet?

I replied that I wasn't his type. And he wasn't the kind of writer who preyed on literary acolytes. He wasn't like those Casanovas of American creative writing programs who view sex as one of the perks of the profession. He wasn't always receptive, even to those who propositioned him. He once recounted how Brad Davis, fresh from stardom in the film *Midnight Express*, had crawled on hands and knees across the floor of Gore's apartment and begged to blow him. This was a total turnoff, he said. Uninterested in sex with his social or financial or creative equals, he preferred rent boys, rough trade, guys who trailed ragged edges of danger that he believed he could tame with cash.

(Gore later told a friend a totally different story about Brad Davis, claiming he had sex with the young actor on the floor of a bathroom at the Chateau Marmont Hotel in L.A. Davis died in 1991 in an assisted suicide.)

Surprisingly few of the men Gore socialized with in Rome shared his sexual predilections. Other than Howard, the one gay Gore saw regularly was George Armstrong, a bald, soft-spoken journalist from Little Rock via Harvard University. Pressed to survive as a freelancer, Armstrong supplemented his income as a stringer for English and American newspapers by typing Gore's manuscripts and editing dialogue for the documentaries Gore narrated. While Vidal's biographer would later mention that the two men sometimes traveled together, "especially to the Italian cities they were both enchanted by," he neglected to add that much of their joint enchantment consisted of trips to Stazione Termini, cruising for trade.

Such forays were among Rome's enduring attractions for Gore. I had been present during his interview with Barbara Grizzuti Harrison, who coaxed him into describing the city's special appeal. A heavyset woman with serious respiratory problems that made stair climbing a calvary, Harrison had an endearing confidence that every Italian man she encountered was flirting with her. She couldn't conceive that anyone did not view the country as she did—and as do those dreamy postcard photographers who airbrush out of their snapshots all garbage and beggars and pariah dogs.

"Is it the colors that you love?" she asked. "Is it the quality of the light? Is it the warmth of the people?"

"Well, what I like—you have to understand I came here shortly after World War II," Gore deadpanned. "What I like is you could go up to the Pincio at night and buy any boy you wanted for five hundred lire."

That quotation didn't make it into Harrison's book *Italian Days*.

Gore called the boys he picked up "bunnies." Howard called them "faygalas," or little birds. But the ones I noticed seemed anything except soft, downy, and harmless. They were butch guys who consented to have sex for money, all the while denying that they usually did this sort of thing.

In those days Gore worked out at a gym on Via Barberini and believed he could handle the situation if a trick turned greedy or aggressive. Howard, too, liked to give the impression that he knew how to take care of himself. But then their bravado, along with the equanimity of the city, was shattered by a grotesque murder.

The evening of November 3, 1975, I arrived at their apartment

to discover Gore and Howard in a grim discussion of the day's flab-
bergasting headline. Pier Paolo Pasolini had been killed and his
body mutilated on a desolate beach at Ostia, the ancient seaport
outside Rome. Police had arrested a seventeen-year-old boy who
was accused of stealing Pasolini's Alfa Romeo and running over
his corpse several times before speeding away. Although he confessed to the killing, Giuseppe Pelosi swore he had acted in self-
defense. He said Pasolini had picked him up at the train station
and promised money for sex, a commonplace exchange both for
the kid and for the celebrated poet, novelist, filmmaker, and po-
lemicist. But Pelosi testified that when Pasolini attempted to sod-
omize him with a stick, he fought back. (In the following decades
Pelosi recanted the story—but that is another endless Roman tale.)

Gore didn't need to acknowledge out loud anything so banal as
that he could have been the one who was dead on the beach. Not
only had the homicidal hustler been spawned in his favorite hunting ground, not only had the pick-up replicated hundreds of his
sexual arrangements, but the victim had been an acquaintance of
Gore's. In fact, at the age of fifty-three, Pasolini might well have
been Gore's doppelgänger, and what Italo Calvino had written
about Pasolini could have applied to Vidal as well: he was "the ide-
ologizer of eros and the eroticizer of ideology."

Equally at home in literature and film, in high life and low,
Pasolini had for decades been an omnipresent cultural figure in
Italy. Writing for newspapers and magazines, producing plays and
documentaries, appearing on TV, participating in political rallies,
he was a controversial personality and the target of strident cen-
sorship by the government and the Catholic Church. While his
same-sex orientation was blatant, he, like Gore, resisted categori-
zation. Athletic and histrionically virile, he was attached to his
mother and to Italy's cult of *mammismo*. Also like Gore, who had
been stigmatized since his mid-twenties for the publication of his
homosexually themed novel *The City and the Pillar*, Pasolini had
early in his career been fired from a teaching job in his provincial

hometown and charged with the corruption of minors and having sex with male students.

Fleeing to Rome, he joined the Communist Party but couldn't abide the party line. He expended as much energy on poetry as on politics and compiled a popular anthology of verse in regional dialects. With the rise of student activism in the 1960s and 1970s, he separated himself from those who regarded the young demonstrators as revolutionaries. Instead, he sided with the policemen, whom he viewed as the true proletariat, poor refugees largely from the south who were ordered into the streets to control pampered college kids, the sons and daughters of the bourgeoisie.

This stance was an extension of his interest—and his sexual involvement—in the life of the brutally ugly *borgate* on Rome's periphery. His first novel, *Ragazzi di vita* (published in 1955), dealt with the sorts of marginalized boys of irrepressible spirits and limited prospects whom he played soccer with. It was just such a boy who killed him. His first movie, *Accatone* (1961), based on his novel *A Violent Life* (1959), also focused on petty criminals from the disenfranchised underclass. This work, like many of his subsequent books and films—*Teorema* (1968), *The Decameron* (1971), *The Canterbury Tales* (1972), *Arabian Nights* (1974), and his final movie, *Salò, or the 120 Days of Sodom* (1975)—prompted legal charges for obscenity and sexual perversion.

If he had shrill critics, he also had influential defenders who admired his political commitment, his artistic talent, and his shrewd analysis of Italy's crises of consumerism and corruption. But Pasolini never appeared to comprehend that his behavior might compromise the message of his work or that after he rescued boys from the *borgate*, it might strike some as exploitative to have sex with them. In his defense, he could have pointed to the lasting relationship and creative partnership he had with Ninetto Davoli, a fifteen-year-old who went on to feature in seven of Pasolini's films. But Giuseppe Pelosi was probably more typical of his partners.

Pasolini's killer was tried and sentenced to nine years in prison.

The court accepted Pelosi's plea of mitigating circumstances and took into consideration his youth. The verdict did little to end debate about the case. From the first, Gore and Howard, along with millions of Italians, refused to accept at face value police reports or media accounts of the murder. They rejected out of hand Pelosi's contention that he had agreed to have sex but had defended himself against being sodomized with a stick. "He was peddling his ass," Vidal said, "plain and simple." For them Pelosi's age and poverty and Pasolini's wealth and prominence were nonfactors.

Nor did Gore and Howard view the murder as a cautionary event that should have changed their routine. There was no chance they would stop cruising Termini. Instead, they joined the general clamor for an alternative explanation, a theory that wove together disparate threads, revealing a tapestry of official lies and political skulduggery.

This national tendency, known as dietrology, promulgated the belief that supposedly self-evident facts are often illusory and that the truth lies beneath the surface of a bogus scenario concocted to protect the guilty and aggrandize the powerful. Rumors circulated that Giuseppe Pelosi was actually a street thug hired by persons unknown to eliminate Pasolini for reasons unexplained. Alternately, Pelosi hadn't even been the killer, just a fall guy for fascists or communists or Catholics or Mafia gangsters who had their separate, or perhaps mutual, motives for killing Pasolini. After his parole from prison, Pelosi continued to tell different versions of Pasolini's death, none of which overturned his guilty verdict.

All these counter-narratives confirmed Gore's confidence in his talent for sniffing out plots, including those against him. Indeed, his suspicion that Pasolini must have been assassinated by political opponents or mysterious enemies fed his fear that he, too, was a target for forces out to destroy him. He claimed he often received death threats. When told that this sounded a tad paranoid, he replied, "Anybody who's not paranoid is not in full possession of the facts."

•

Oscar Wilde proclaimed that a bad review might spoil his breakfast but never his lunch. In the same spirit, Vidal refused to let Pasolini's murder ruin that Roman autumn. Along with the rest of us, he enjoyed the last few nights of alfresco dining—nights steeped in the aroma of wood smoke, olive oil, and roasting chestnuts. At a restaurant on Piazza del Popolo we watched a party of eight pass around a truffle the size of a man's fist, each diner inhaling deeply as if to hold in mind the earthy scent of the season.

Then the weather broke with the abrupt emphasis of a slammed door, and overnight it was winter. Weeds sprouted between cobblestones, and green moss veined white marble slabs. Statues along Via dei Fori Imperiali were gloved in gray lichen and shod in dead leaves. The metal flanges that propped up walls in the Forum bled rust like pitons left behind by mountain climbers.

Gore's new novel, *1876*, was due out in March. Another of his historical blockbusters, a sequel to *Burr*, it resumed the story of Charles Schuyler, who returns to the States after decades in Europe to file news reports about the presidential election and to angle for an ambassadorial appointment for himself and a husband for his daughter. *Time* magazine planned to feature Vidal on its cover, prompting Gore to dub himself "a third-generation celebrity," certified by the fact that his grandfather and father had made the cover of *Time* before him.

Meanwhile, *Texas Monthly* assigned me to review Tennessee Williams's *Memoirs*, and when Gore heard that I had a copy of the galleys, he urged me to pass it along. He intended to write about it for *The New York Review of Books*. That he should have recused himself because of his long friendship with Williams never crossed his mind. This, I inferred, was the way the game was played at the top level. Punctiliousness about such matters applied only to mid-listers like me who were instructed to step aside as reviewers if we had so much as a passing acquaintance with an author, his agent, or his publisher.

Not that I mentioned this to Gore. Heading off to Largo Argentina to deliver the galleys, I welcomed a get-together that didn't revolve around drinks and dinner and a sprawling cast of supporting characters. I hoped he and I would have a chance to discuss the merits of Williams's memoir, which I thought silly and shallow and, in spots, cringe-makingly bad.

I arrived to find Gore being interviewed by Alvin Shuster of the *Los Angeles Times*. I offered to leave, but he signaled for me to stay. Seldom averse to an audience, he put on a splendid performance, repeating quotations that I had heard him polish for months. Some of these lines stuck in the mind like song lyrics—what came to be known as ear worms. His dictum that "the brain that doesn't feed itself eats itself" had been perfected into "the mind that doesn't nourish itself devours itself." When asked by Shuster to predict who would win the Democratic nomination for the presidency in 1980, he trotted out a quip that needed no improving. "Teddy Kennedy. Every declining culture deserves a King Farouk."

It didn't disappoint me that many of Vidal's memorable sound bites were the products of practice. It showed how much of his success, which seemed effortless, depended on hard work. But that wasn't to say he didn't excel at spontaneous wit as well.

On an evening in 1989, when Francis Ford Coppola was in Rome shooting *The Godfather: Part III*, Mickey Knox, who had a bit part in the film, threw a party for the cast and crew and cooked up a batch of his fabled meatless, beanless chili. Gore was among the guests, and because I had rewritten a short scene for the script, Mickey invited me as an afterthought.

Gore and I were sitting together on a couch, idly spooning up brown mush, when a handsome young man in blue jeans sauntered over. His face looked familiar, but I didn't catch his name and only afterward learned that he was Andy Garcia.

"Sorry to interrupt," he said. "But before I leave, I wanted to say hello to my favorite author."

Gore extended his hand with the practiced solemnity of a cardinal presenting his ring to be kissed.

"I don't mean you," Garcia said. "I mean Mr. Mewshaw."

This had all the earmarks of one of Mickey Knox's elephantine jokes—a double-edged gag to tweak Gore's nose and at the same time embarrass me. Guardedly, I asked, "What have you read of mine?"

"I don't read much," Garcia conceded. "I have an awful lot of scripts to get through, and I'm sort of dyslexic. But I saw a funny article you wrote about eating with your kids at the first McDonald's in Rome, and I think that's the best thing I've ever read."

Andy Garcia shook my hand and exited stage left. It was a moment to treasure. Even though he hadn't read my books, in this company it was heartening to hear that I was his favorite author.

Gore promptly put an end to my preening. "You can have all the dyslexic ones."

After Alvin Shuster finished the interview and departed, I handed Tennessee Williams's *Memoirs* to Gore and offered my opinion. "It's terrible. A very tired performance."

In three-quarter profile, he crooked an eyebrow, as he habitually did when doling out discipline. "Homophobia?"

"I couldn't care less about his sexual preferences," I said. "It's the insipid way he expresses them that turned me off." I quoted a sample of Williams's prose. "'As you may have gathered at this point, I fall in love rather easily, and the ease is easier when the object is warm, willing and "a joy forever."'"

"Well, it hasn't helped the Glorious Bird's style that he's been hitting the sauce and the pills all these years."

We sat for a moment in silence. The *salone* was as coldly

uncomfortable as my spartan quarters at the American Academy. Because Italians like to pretend that winter doesn't exist, freezing weather always comes to them as a shock. But the greater shock to me was that a millionaire like Gore couldn't keep his apartment heated.

Early on he and I had established that we shared an upbringing in Washington, D.C., albeit on different sides, and in markedly different social strata, of the city. My family, resolutely blue-collar, joined the white flight from the integrated downtown and raised me in Prince George's County, Maryland, in a precinct described by one sociologist as "America's first suburban slum."

Because Gore's kin regarded even the Kennedys as bog-trotting arrivistes, he had no reluctance to razz me about my Irish Catholicism. "I guess you were one of those Gonzaga boys. They all had terrible acne."

"Wrong on both counts," I fired back. "I went to DeMatha, and I had a perfect complexion." Gonzaga, I pointed out, was a Jesuit high school that graduated droves of white-shoe lawyers, diplomats, and politicians. DeMatha was famous for its athletes and the large number of basketball and football players it sent to college and on to the pros.

As much as Gore enjoyed ribbing me about my humble ancestry and his blue blood, I never believed that he really cared what background I came from. At the end of that afternoon, he gave me a copy of *1876*, signed it, and said, "Someday this will be worth ten dollars"—the list price of the hardback.

That spring, *The New York Review of Books* ran more than five thousand words of his reaction to Williams's *Memoirs*. Slowly circling his subject, Gore began by summarizing the portrait of Williams that had appeared in previous autobiographies by Paul Bowles and Harold Acton. Acton drew his ire for mocking Tennessee's indifference to Italian culture and to the well-being of the boys he dallied with. Perhaps with Pasolini's murder still in mind, Vidal switched the accusation around: "Italian trade has never had much interest in the character, aspirations, or desires of those to whom they rent their ass."

Then in deft thrusts he skewered several of Tennessee's close friends. "The best that one could say of [Anna] Magnani was that she liked dogs." While conceding that Carson McCullers was "artistically gifted," Vidal called her "humanly appalling." He reserved his most venomous scorn for Truman Capote, who, he wrote, resembled a miniature gargoyle, yet seemed to believe that "the very sight of him was enough to cause lifelong heterosexual men to tumble out of unsuspected closets."

As he shifted his full attention to Tennessee Williams, Gore became part rhapsodizer, part raptor. He fondly recalled old times together—nights prowling for boys in Paris, an expedition by jeep to the Amalfi coast, early days when Williams was the sun and Gore a faint planet in the surrounding constellation. Although their respective literary status gradually changed, Gore never denigrated his friend's achievement or lost sight of the hounding he suffered from homophobes. But neither did he shy away from the primary causes of the playwright's decline. Even before Tennessee fell under the sway of booze and pills, he was, Gore observed, prone to bouts of self-pity, "flapping what looks like a pathetically broken wing," impersonating Judy Garland in her late, least attractive days, a masochist simultaneously attracting and fighting off sadists. Alcohol only exaggerated the rot that was already apparent.

The greatest tragedy, as Gore saw it, was Tennessee's abuse of his talent. He described him as solipsistic to a fatal degree, "indifferent to place, art, history. Bird seldom reads a book and the only history he knows is his own; he depends, finally, on romantic genius to get him through life." By contrast, Gore characterized himself as a "compulsive learner of new things."

In a variant on his koan that the mind that doesn't nourish itself devours itself, he concluded, "Tennessee is the sort of writer who does not develop; he simply continues. By the time he was an adolescent he had his themes. Constantly he plays and replays the same small but brilliant set of cards. I am not aware that any new information (or feeling?) has got through to him in the twenty-eight years since our Roman spring."

It was difficult to conceive of a more devastating put-down of a fellow writer, a friend no less. So much for my notion that Gore was too close to Williams to file an honest review.

That he might have been speaking not just *for* himself but *to* himself didn't occur to me until much later when I realized Gore feared that the Great Wheel of Fortune would turn against him as it had against Tennessee, and for the same reasons. Not that he would have acknowledged any of this back then. As *1876* shot to the top of the bestseller list and brought him to the States for what seemed more like a coast-to-coast political campaign than a publicity tour, there was only one thing that tarnished his triumph. Soon after *Time* published its cover story on her son, Nina sent the magazine a poison-pen letter, excoriating Gore for ingratitude. She had, she insisted, played a crucial role in his success and believed the record should reflect that her influence had launched his career, kept him out of harm's way during World War II, and set him up in the film business.

After trimming Nina's screed to manageable length, *Time* printed it under the headline "Mother's Love." Gore would maintain a stony silence toward Nina for the rest of her life.

THREE

After another term at the University of Texas, Linda and I and our son, Sean, now two years old, returned to Rome in 1977, again at the invitation of the American Academy. We took up residence at the Villa Chiaraviglio, palatial accommodations compared with our previous digs. The place had a kitchen the size of an operating theater, a living room with a wood-burning fireplace, and vaulted ceilings that soared to a height of twenty feet. Double French doors opened onto a brick-paved terrace in back, and beyond that flourished a garden of palms, citrus trees, and oleanders that a team of topiary artists had pruned into precise geometric shapes.

A gravel path of white pebbles—each one appeared to have been set in place by hand—ran parallel to an aqueduct that fed the Fontanone dell'Acqua Paola, which Eleanor Clark described in *Rome and a Villa* as "the baroque at its most loving and serene." From in front of the fountain a landscape of campaniles, arches, lanterns, and loggias undulated toward the Alban Hills like a vast lesson from an architecture manual.

With the city somnolently baptized in dense golden light, I wondered whether it was pollen that created this lovely pointillism. Or was it pollution? Whichever, Italy was far from as peaceful as it appeared from our perch on the Gianicolo. Journalists christened that era the *anni di piombo*, years of lead, and the label stuck. Waging war against a sclerotic political system, radical cells had gone underground and launched murderous guerrilla raids against the police, corporate executives, and elected officials.

The most vicious of these urban terrorist bands, the Red Brigades, fought under the banner of *tanto peggio, tanto meglio*—so much the worse, so much the better—and attacked the Communist Party for rejecting revolution in favor of respectability, for propping up the Christian Democrats rather than destroying them. The Red Brigades especially detested the proposed "historical compromise" between the two parties. Hoping to provoke a backlash from the government, it daubed graffiti on walls throughout Rome. "Violence is the coagulant of the movement's subjective energy." "The machine gun is beautiful." "So long as the violence of the state is called justice, the justice of the people will be called violence."

Even the American Academy, in its palmy isolation, wasn't spared. During the annual spring show, a smoke bomb cleared the building and closed the exhibition. But this was small beer compared with what befell factories and universities up and down the peninsula. Labor disputes and student demonstrations degenerated into riots. There were bombings, kidnappings, kneecappings, and assassinations.

Still, despite alarming press dispatches that made Rome sound as dangerous as Belfast or Beirut, life continued there much as it always had. Although *The New Yorker* reported that after dark nobody ventured outdoors "except for muggers and nervous bachelors walking their new Dobermans," every piazza teemed with the familiar commedia dell'arte. All the best restaurants and cafés were crammed to the rafters, many of them with foreign correspondents who, after an evening of partying, posted stories that described a city under siege. When I asked Gore Vidal his opinion of these apocalyptic reports, he replied that "a revolution in Italy is about as likely as a pogrom in Tahiti."

I should have kept in mind that he, as long as he had lived here, had never been truly engaged by the Italian scene. Given his interest in America's national security apparatus and its overseas intelligence operations, he should have been riveted by revelations that the United States had financed the Christian Democratic Party and undermined the Communists, paying off journalists and subsidizing an English-language newspaper, the *Daily American*, as a mouthpiece for the U.S. embassy's point of view. But in none of his essays, in no interview, and certainly in no novel did he ever address the topic of Italian student protest, workers' grievances, or terrorism. His second memoir, *Point to Point Navigation*, whose chronology coincides with the *anni di piombo*, mentioned the Red Brigades just twice, and one of those was to joke about Federico Fellini, who confessed to a fear of being kidnapped because "I am too large to fit into the boot of a car."

No, Gore Vidal, like a lot of expats—I don't exclude myself—treated Italy as a luxury hotel he could check into and out of as it pleased him. But blind to that and a lot of other things in 1977, I pitched *Harper's* an article which would stress that news accounts about the Red Brigades needed to be put into perspective. More people were murdered in random violence over an average weekend in Houston or Washington, D.C., than Italian terrorists killed in a year. The editor Lewis Lapham liked the idea, and I went to work.

Which is to say I went to lunch with economists and sociologists, counterterrorism experts and embassy officials. Among my "sources" were American journalists in town to cover the country's collapse and simultaneously enjoy its age-old attractions. None of us ever actually encountered a bloody-clawed, fully fanged, free-range terrorist. A few Italian reporters who attempted to contact the Red Brigades had had their kneecaps blown off. One was shot point-blank in the head and left to die in front of his wife. That sort of hard-core field research called for a much higher kill fee than *Harper's* had promised me. I felt I was fulfilling my contract by roving the streets of Rome, letting it all wash over me—scenes of boys playing soccer under the portico of the Pantheon, enterprising old men painting grids on the cobblestones and pretending to be parking lot attendants, young lovers kissing, then stretching out full length on the ledge in front of Palazzo Farnese, persuaded of their impregnability under the bored gaze of armed guards at the French embassy.

During that period of political turmoil, Gore Vidal published *Matters of Fact and of Fiction: Essays, 1973–1976* and debated what to do about *Kalki*, a novel that his editor at Random House, Jason Epstein, found strange and unsettling and in need of a comprehensive rewrite. Vidal conveyed his distress about this to me and our mutual agent, Owen Laster, on a flawless autumn afternoon as he led us on a guided tour of classical sites. At the Theater of Marcellus, Palazzo Orsini clung like a clam to the inner shell of the ancient amphitheater, and its rooms had been divided into private apartments. Gore mused that many years earlier he had been offered an end unit with a princely terrace for the bargain price of thirty thousand dollars. Now he had regrets—over opportunities lost, false economies, the unreliability of his judgment. With his mood vacillating between melancholy and waspish irritation, he had earlier confided to me that he was losing faith in Owen Laster, whom he referred to as "a little faggot too weak to stand up to Jason."

Days later he and Owen and Howard flew to New York and attended a party at Lally Weymouth's where Gore got into a fight with Norman Mailer—"the night of small fists," he called it. This, too, was a source of regret, and when he returned to Rome, he admitted that he, no less than Mailer, had behaved like a buffoon. Although he continued to disagree with Jason Epstein about *Kalki*, he quit complaining about Owen Laster's lack of backbone and buckled down to rewrite the novel.

In the spring of 1978, Linda and I invited him and Howard

to dinner at the Villa Chiaraviglio to meet the new director of the American Academy, John D'Arms—the name rhymed with "gendarmes"—and his wife, Teresa, the daughter of Evelyn Waugh. Donald and Luisa Stewart rounded out the table along with the novelist Mary Lee Settle, who had just won the National Book Award for *Blood Tie*.

Linda prudently hired somebody to help with Sean, a boisterous and precociously verbal kid. But after the babysitter bathed him and read him a bedtime story, Sean refused to stay in his room. He kept running and sliding on the marble floors in his footed pajamas, squealing, "I want to meet Gore Vee-doll! I want to meet Gore Vee-doll!"

Linda and he struck a bargain. If he quieted down, he could stay up to say hello to Gore Vidal. After that, he had to go to sleep. In an overstuffed chair, his blond mop of hair red-tinged by firelight, he sat with his legs stretched to the edge of a cushion. When the D'Armses showed up, he barely acknowledged their presence. He had started nodding off, his head wobbling on the skinny stalk of his neck.

Then Mary Lee Settle arrived and told us she had known Gore back in the 1950s, when she taught at Bard College and he and Howard lived at Edgewater, their Georgian home on the Hudson River. She recalled him affectionately as a young man, neither as cocksure nor as lordly as he was now. In fact, she said, he had been the butt of jokes by older writers who, far from afraid of his barbs, zinged him with their own. She remembered Gore declaring to Delmore Schwartz, "I've just had an epiphany," and Schwartz quipping, "Have you been masturbating again?"

Not much interested in literary gossip, Sean maintained his drowsy vigil. Then, when Gore and Howard finally showed up, he snapped wide awake.

Notoriously indifferent to kids, Gore was nevertheless so often asked to act as a godfather he had honed a line he would reprise for generations. "Always a godfather, never a god." He bestowed a thin smile on Sean. "Aren't you a pretty little girl."

"I'm a boy," Sean protested.

"Well, then, aren't you a pretty little boy."

"Gore Vee-doll," Sean chirped.

Pleased that a child knew his name, Gore leaned down to the pretty little boy, who declaimed in clearly enunciated syllables, "I want to eat you."

The reaction . . . There was none. Everybody froze. At a loss for words, reduced to dumb miming, Gore wiggled his ears, then performed a trick that made it appear that he had detached the last joint from his thumb. This set Sean giggling, and the rest of us joined in, laughing in relief.

While Linda bundled Sean off to bed, I poured Gore a glass of white wine and Howard a vodka on the rocks. Gore surprised me, saying he, too, wanted vodka. Had Sean's remark rattled him that badly?

At dinner, Donald Stewart urged Mary Lee Settle to tell us about the National Book Award. Tall and striking, she had once been a model and still carried herself at sixty with a stylish panache. Strolling with me through Trastevere, she had sidestepped thunderous motor scooters, delighted that the drivers all shot her admiring glances. In my eagerness not to get run over, I hadn't noticed this.

Mary Lee was later quoted as claiming that winning the National Book Award was "one of the most unpleasant experiences I have ever had." But that night she was ebullient and explained that *Blood Tie* had at first been published to near-total silence. Few reviews, paltry sales. Then Anatole Broyard had written an enthusiastic notice in the daily *New York Times*, and Settle's good friend Vance Bourjaily, a member of the fiction jury, used the review to persuade the other National Book Award judges to vote for her. "It was a miracle," Mary Lee marveled. "*The New York Times* hadn't reviewed me for thirteen years."

"That's the way of the Great Gray Goose," said Gore, gulping down a second vodka. "After *The City and the Pillar*, the *Times* refused to review my next six books." He recited their titles like the Sorrowful Mysteries of the rosary—*The Season of Comfort*; *A Search for the King*; *Dark Green, Bright Red*; *The Judgment of Paris*; *Messiah*; *A Thirsty Evil*. From the way he talked, you'd never know that his taboo-breaking novel had had its advocates. Thomas Mann had hailed it as "a noble work."

Howard, hyperalert to trouble, urged Gore to switch to wine. Gore demanded more vodka.

"It's interesting how alcohol affects different writers," he said, as if that were what we had been discussing—alcohol and authors. "Whenever I read Faulkner and he rambles on about 'the ancient avatar of the evening sun slipping down the crepuscular sky,' I know he was hitting the sauce. On the other hand, your sainted father," he said, nodding to Teresa Waugh D'Arms, "became meaner and more concise the drunker he got. Every sentence had a dagger in it."

When Mary Lee Settle began waxing sentimental about their days on the Hudson River, Gore brought up the names of several men at Bard College and asked if she had slept with them after he had.

"Time to go home," Howard broke in. With no protest, Gore pitched unsteadily to his feet, and the two of them departed.

The next day he phoned to deliver a line that he doubtlessly wished he had thought of when Sean announced he wanted to eat him. "Who was that dwarf you hired to get the evening off to such a rousing start?"

It had been a dinner party distinguished by firsts—first time we entertained Gore and Howard at our place; first time I saw Vidal speechless; first time I saw him drunk in public. But foremost it was the first time I recognized the key role Howard Austen played in his life. To paraphrase Hillary Clinton, he wasn't just some little wifey who stood by his man and stayed at home baking cookies. Nor was he like Tennessee Williams's great love, Frank Merlo, who, when asked by the American ambassador in Rome what he did, perkily replied, "Oh, I just fuck Mr. Williams."

Howard Austen was a substantial figure in his own right, and his relationship with Gore survived for more than half a century because, if you believed them, they didn't have sex. Which wasn't to say that they had never had sex. They bumped into each other in New York's Everard Baths on Labor Day 1950, and after what Howard described as a disastrous bout in bed, they stayed together and struck up what amounted to a *mariage blanc*.

Not that *blanc* in their case signified a chaste life. There was always plenty of sex, and according to those who knew them well, while they might not have made love to each other, strictly speaking, they traded partners back and forth and sometimes had sex with the same partner at the same time.

Regardless of the intricacies of their intimate lives, they settled in as long-term partners when Gore was just twenty-five and Howard twenty-one. Friendship was paramount, but both were very practical fellows. Officially, Howard worked for Gore and received a salary—seventy-five thousand dollars a year back in the days when that amount was the maximum that qualified under the U.S. overseas tax exclusion. And he earned every penny of it, managing Vidal's complex financial affairs, booking their travel, and looking after various residences. In addition to the rented apartment in Rome, Gore owned a brownstone in New York City and a magnificent villa in Ravello on the Amalfi coast. Then, in 1978, he bought a house on Outpost Drive in Los Angeles's Hollywood Hills. All of them required attention, but overseeing the villa in Ravello, according to Donald Stewart, an experienced yachtsman, was "like maintaining an ocean liner. Every year you have to chip and repaint it starting from the stern, and by the time you reach the bow, you have to go back and begin again." It fell to Howard to hire and ride herd on the painters, the groundskeepers, the cook, the cleaning girl, the battalions of repairmen.

The house in the Hollywood Hills was frequently rented, and Howard vetted prospective tenants and attended to the upkeep and to the cleaning before new occupants moved in. He also haggled with accountants over California state taxes, U.S. federal taxes, and the ticklish question, finessed whenever possible, of Italian taxes.

If he had had his choice, Howard would have lived most of the year in L.A. He liked the glitz and the gossip. As a young man, he had harbored dreams of a show business career and had been a stage manager for several Broadway plays and helped cast the film version of *To Kill a Mockingbird*. His secret ambition was to become a pop singer. But he suffered mortal stage fright. Still, he had a soulful tenor voice, and despite his emphysema, exacerbated by chain-smoking, he would break out at dinner parties with a cappella renditions of show tunes and torch songs.

Howard decried the decline in attractiveness of current Hollywood leading men, complaining that most of them were character actors, not true stars. "A star," he instructed me, "is somebody you couldn't in your wildest wet dream imagine fucking. Character actors are people you know you could fuck."

Judgmental as he was on this score, he had no inflated notion of his own sexual allure. "My trouble," he told a friend of mine, "is I'm nobody's type." Still, he made the best of what he had, joined Gore for the occasional nip and tuck of cosmetic surgery, and dyed his formerly red hair a sandy color.

He adamantly disapproved of my hair. Having gone salt-and-pepper gray in my twenties, and solid white by my mid-thirties, I imagined myself as distinguished looking. Howard disagreed. "You just look old." He showed me a photograph of their friend Paul Newman, whose hair was white and close-cropped. "If you won't dye it, at least cut it short. That's what Paul does, and it takes years off his age."

Howard often badgered Gore about his appearance, especially his monotonous wardrobe. Sometimes he tried a positive approach and insisted that Gore had excellent taste in clothing. He simply hated to shop. But nothing he said could persuade Gore to forsake his rumpled blue blazer, gray trousers, and beat-up shoes.

At the start of their life together, Gore had wisecracked that Howard was his child. But over the decades, their roles reversed. Now Howard monitored Gore's drinking, admonished him for his inflammatory remarks, and generally attempted to keep him from slipping off the rails. To those of us looking on, it sometimes seemed Howard had limited success as a surrogate Jewish mother. But when he wasn't around, and later when he was gone for good, we were forced to acknowledge how herculean Howard's efforts had been.

The question of what Howard derived from the relationship apart from a salary and first-class perks has no easy answer. Some people were satisfied that he loved Gore; some suspected he had to be a masochist to accept the abuse. Neither explanation struck me as adequate. Then, reading Jean Genet's *The Thief's Journal*, I stumbled upon a passage that might have come out of Howard's mouth. "I was the valet whose job was to look after, to dust, polish and wax, an object of great value which, however, through the miracle of friendship, belonged to me . . . The more I obeyed serious orders, the greater was my intimacy with him who issued them."

In December 1977, I delivered my article "Two Cheers for Italy" to *Harper's*. It was quickly set in galleys and scheduled for publication in the February 1978 issue. But after I corrected the page proofs, Lewis Lapham insisted I revise the piece and shorten it by 50 percent. Then he decreed he would pay one thousand dollars, instead of the agreed-upon fee of three thousand dollars.

I asked Gore for advice. Instead of recommending that I hold

Harper's to its contract, he counseled me to do as Lapham demanded. Better that, he reasoned, than have the article killed. He assured me he was no stranger to rough treatment by magazines. Some of his best essays, such as "The Holy Family," a gimlet-eyed glance at the Kennedys, and "Pink Triangle and Yellow Star," a depiction of homosexuals and Jews as equal victims of prejudice, had started off as assignments from *The New York Review of Books* but were rejected and wound up appearing elsewhere. Who was I to imagine myself immune from professional realities?

In that pre-Internet era, when mail took weeks to cross the Atlantic to Italy and few editors would waste money phoning a freelancer, I learned after the fact that the February issue of *Harper's* didn't carry my article. When the March issue hit the newsstands, friends informed me the piece didn't appear in that one either. Only at the end of the month, after Aldo Moro, the former prime minister, had been kidnapped by the Red Brigades, did I hear from Lewis Lapham that he had shelved "Two Cheers for Italy" until the situation resolved itself.

Fifty-four days later, on May 9, 1978, I was on a bus, stalled in traffic just beyond Ponte Garibaldi. Cars and pedestrians clotted the streets in all directions. Another *manifestazione* of striking workers or student demonstrators, I assumed. When I jumped off the bus, however, I heard the crowd murmur a single word. "Moro," they whispered. "Moro. Moro."

Gleaning snippets of information, I advanced on foot through the thronged Jewish ghetto. Police had discovered Moro's body in a Renault parked on Via Caetani. For fear that the corpse might be booby-trapped, the carabinieri struggled to keep mourners and gawkers at a distance. But I pressed through the maze of medieval alleys to Piazza Mattei, where men and women climbed atop the Fontana delle Tartarughe and clung to the statues of naked bronze boys hoisting bronze turtles over their shoulders into a brimming basin. Whenever challenged by the police, I flashed my credentials for the upcoming Italian Open tennis tournament, a card marked *Stampa* (Press), and slowly edged within yards of a priest who was bent over the back of the Renault administering the last rites.

Journalistic accounts and dozens of subsequent books reported that for symbolic purposes the Red Brigades deposited Moro's body equidistant between the Communist and the Christian Democratic party headquarters, condemning both groups for negotiating a "historic compromise." In fact, the car was in front of the American Studies Center, and if there was symbolism, it could be seen as a bloody thumb in the eye of the United States for its constant intrusion into Italian affairs.

After the priest finished and a forensic team commenced processing the scene, I stayed on, noting everything down to minute and incongruous details. A street vendor lugging buckets of olives and garbanzo beans decided this was a perfect place to do business. Angry mobs chased him away. They had tears in their eyes, as did the women arranging sprays of flowers against the wall behind the Renault.

Another month passed before *Harper's* notified me that "Two Cheers for Italy" couldn't be published unless I completely reconceived it, taking into account Moro's kidnapping and assassination, its causes and implications for the future of the country. Because the magazine had held the article until it was outdated by events, I thought it fair to ask to be paid for a rewrite. *Harper's* dismissed this idea and me with a swiftness that indicated no desire for further communication.

While I licked my wounds, *The New York Times* called to discuss an article about the Red Brigades. Not, it was emphasized, the sort of scissors-and-paste rehash most newspapers carried. The *Times Magazine* suggested I penetrate a terrorist cell and file a story from the inside—"to show the human face behind the terrorist mask."

This was a joke, a cruel and dangerous one in which mention

of a kill fee amounted to the sickest sort of black humor. Not a single intelligence agent, much less a freelance hack, had ever infiltrated a Red Brigades *covo*.

"That's the beauty of it," the *Times* editor said. "It's never been done before. You do it and an article's just the beginning. You'll get a book contract, maybe a movie deal."

"Why not give the assignment to your bureau chief?" I said, knowing full well Henry Kamm would reject the idea as ridiculous.

"Don't say no until you've thought it over. All the time you've spent in Italy, you must have sources."

"I wouldn't know where to start or who to ask."

After a pause, the editor posed a tantalizing question. "Well, who knows any more about the Red Brigades than you do?"

The question stuck in my brain like a burr, just as did memories of those days in Rome, my evolving picture of Gore Vidal, and my impression that he, like the city, concealed his deepest secrets behind an elaborate facade.

FOUR

After my misfortunes with *Harper's*, followed by the train wreck of an assignment from *Playboy*—Donald Stewart arranged for me to write an article about Graham Greene that got rejected, later appeared in *The Nation,* and was then plagiarized by Penelope Gilliatt in *The New Yorker*—a wiser man might have chosen to stick to fiction. But this was the heyday of New Journalism's noisy ascendancy, when lots of authors were hustling for magazine work, hoping to tap into a broader vein of readers and increase the audience for their novels. I drafted a proposal to do a profile of Gore Vidal, one that would counter the cliché portrait of him as an icy, mean-spirited, America-hating, narcissistic sexual deviate.

He himself had wryly observed in an essay that current literary conventions dictated "what matters is not if a book is good or bad (who after all would know the difference?) but whether or not the author is a good person or a bad person." And because he suffered from a suspect character, his reputation as an artist had suffered. It was time, I suggested, for a reappraisal that would place him in his appropriate context as a politically engaged, socially responsible man of letters in the European mode.

The New York Times Magazine bought the pitch, but Gore was hesitant to cooperate. Convinced that the *Times* would never print anything positive about him, he recounted the tale he often told about Orville Prescott, the daily reviewer, blackballing him in revulsion at the same-sex relationship in *The City and the Pillar*. "You have to keep in mind that it wasn't just the usual fag-baiters who were after me," Vidal added. "During the McCarthy era I was viewed as a dangerously outspoken leftist—not only a threat to the sanctity of the American family, but out to destroy the Republic. When I began spending time in Italy, that inflamed suspicions all the more. I mean, what kind of real man and real American would want to live anywhere except the home of the brave and the land of the free?"

I argued that times and *The New York Times* had changed, and finally Gore agreed to be interviewed as long as I abided by several ground rules. First, he instructed me to avoid any mention of his cosmetic surgery. "If you write that I've had my eyes done, it'll be all over the tabloids that my whole face is plastic."

Second, he urged me not to reveal who owned the villa in Ravello. I didn't need to lie, just leave the situation vague, allowing for the possibility that he rented the place. It was nobody's business that he had bought it through a Swiss shell corporation to avoid Italian taxes and create the impression that he was a transient tenant who spent less than half the year in Italy.

Third, and most important, because he was locked in costly litigation with Truman Capote, he insisted on reviewing the manuscript to make sure that it didn't put him in legal jeopardy and undercut his libel claim. This struck me as a sensible precaution. I wanted the article to be accurate and non-actionable. Still, I was adamant that I wouldn't change anything I wrote except for factual errors. My opinions and conclusions had to remain my own.

We arranged to meet in Los Angeles over the 1979 Christmas holidays. Because *The New York Times* provided the princely sum of five hundred dollars in expenses—not enough to pay for airfare, much less a rental car in L.A.—I drove to the West Coast from

Texas and further economized by bunking in a friend's unheated pool house. This was a peculiarity of big-league journalism difficult for a newcomer to comprehend. For the privilege of seeing one's name in print, a freelancer was expected to subsidize the journals he worked for.

Gore's whitewashed, Mediterranean-style mansion on Outpost Drive commanded a crest in the Hollywood Hills, lording it over one of those posh, verdant canyons that make the smoggy flatlands of Southern California feel like a distant planet. On that December day a team of Japanese gardeners was trimming the cypress trees that screened the house from passing traffic. Gore greeted me at the front door wearing his invariable uniform of blue blazer and gray trousers.

"Let me give you the tour," he said, and ushered me around to a patio where the swimming pool used to be. On a terrace, up a flight of steps, a new pool had been installed. Despite the cool, overcast weather, there was a smell of flowers and cut grass and summer. As we gazed across the ultramarine pool toward an expanse of red-tile roofs, he commented, "It's like the setting for a Raymond Chandler murder mystery."

Inside the house the living room was a collision of Andalusia and the Far East, an effusion of Moorish arches and brocade banquettes, Persian carpets, rattan coffee tables, and a Japanese screen. The walls were red, the ceiling a marbled mustard green. Billowing fabric conjured up an impression of what Howard described as "Turkish tents"—a style that he complained was "a bit too effeminate for me." Books and magazines lay scattered about—*The Nation*, William Golding's *Darkness Visible*, *An Illustrated History of the Civil War*, *Jerry Brown Illustrated*, a collection of photographs of China, and a volume titled *L'Amour Bleu*.

Like the decor of his Roman apartment—and like what I later noticed at his villa in Ravello—the overall effect was of a lavishly dressed film set. I felt like an interloper on a stage prepared for a drama whose theme wasn't quite clear. Although Gore always surrounded himself with beautiful furniture and bibelots, he seemed utterly detached from them. He dominated whatever space he occupied; there was no sense that his possessions owned or defined him.

As I set up a tape recorder, Gore avoided eye contact. After thousands of interviews it was inconceivable that he suffered from stage fright. More likely he averted his gaze because of what he imagined he might spot in mine—some inkling of animosity, some intimation that I meant to rake him over the coals first with my questions and later in what I wrote. It cannot be pleasant to realize, as all celebrities must, that the friendliest journalist can mutate into a betrayer or a tormentor.

Snuggling into a chair beside Gore, Rat showed no reluctance to meet my gaze, and under the dog's implacable scrutiny I signaled that I was ready. But Gore jumped up and declared that he craved coffee. In the kitchen he brewed us both a strong cup of Italian espresso. "This stuff has killed more writers than liquor. But I can't live without it," he said.

We rejoined Rat, and when I asked what Gore was working on, his summary of current projects explained why he needed massive infusions of caffeine. He had just finished a draft of *Creation*—fifteen hundred pages in longhand. The novel had required him to master the teachings of Buddha, Confucius, and Zoroaster, and although it was historical fiction, it bore little resemblance to *Burr* and *1876*. Just as had been the case with *Kalki*, Jason Epstein at Random House objected to the book's length and what he perceived as its self-indulgent maundering. He demanded changes and draconian cuts—almost 50 percent of the manuscript. Though annoyed, Gore agreed to comply.

He had also started research on Abraham Lincoln in preparation for a six-hour NBC miniseries. Random House encouraged him to write a novel to tie in with the TV series. Meanwhile, he was completing a script for *Dress Gray*, Lucian Truscott's novel about the murder of a homosexual cadet at West Point, and making notes for a movie about Libby Holman, who had been indicted for shooting her husband, the tobacco heir Zachary Smith Reynolds.

"Why?" I asked. "Why push yourself so hard?"

I anticipated one of his canned answers, some variation on his line about minds needing to nourish themselves. Instead, he acknowledged being depressed. He described middle age as a melancholy period marked by boredom and regret. To hold those demons at bay, he kept busy.

"That contradicts the usual wisdom," I said, "that you're as out of touch with your feelings as you are with the country."

He flashed a wintry smile and held it so long a vertical groove etched his right cheek. While he didn't bother elaborating on his emotions, he denied being out of touch with the United States. "I've studied the nation's history and politics all my life. I fly back every few months. And remember, as co-chairman with Dr. Spock of the People's Party, I whistle-stopped from coast to coast in the early '70s, speaking out against the Vietnam War. I've never considered myself an expatriate. The more I stayed abroad, the more intensely interested I became in the United States, the more clearly I saw it."

He conceded that he had criticized the country. In his opinion, what Americans objected to was that he refused to accept their flattering evaluation of themselves. And he rejected their erroneous assumptions about him. "Americans prefer their writers obscure, poor, and, if possible, doomed by drink or gaudy vice. All the things I'm not."

"Some might consider that statement evidence of egotism and narcissism," I said. "Exactly the sort of thing that puts people off about you."

He tilted his head to one side and treated me to another chilly smile. "Strange. I suppose I'm as egotistical as the next person. But narcissism? In what way? With the exception of *Two Sisters*, I've never drawn directly on my life for fiction. I sometimes talk about myself in essays, but only as a way of acknowledging my point of view. On television I talk about current events or the state of the world. Frankly, I don't find it very interesting to analyze myself."

But didn't his frequent TV appearances create the impression that he was a relentless publicity hound and self-promoter?

"No. Usually I don't even mention my books. I ride my hobby-horses, which tend to concern the commonweal." He reminded me that he once went on the Johnny Carson show carrying a model of an ecologically improved toilet system that could conserve thousands of gallons of water. "What other writer would do that, waste precious airtime when he could be plugging his work?"

I asked whether he actually believed his novels had been ill-treated because of his sexual preferences. Perhaps it was critical rigor, not petty animosity, that had resulted in bad press.

He answered with an anecdote. "When I was nearly broke in the late '40s and early '50s and it became clear I could not get a good review anyplace, I published a series of mysteries under the pseudonym of Edgar Box. All of them were favorably reviewed. But when they were reissued under my name, some of the same magazines that had praised them before were quite negative, even nasty. What would you infer?"

Although it was impossible to gauge how much his career had been damaged, there was little doubt that his attitude toward sex—especially his contention that it's none of the government's business what people do in bed—hadn't helped him. Back when the vogue was for two-fisted authors of irreproachable masculinity, he proclaimed that he was, "like everybody else, bisexual." When fashions changed and an admission of homosexuality might have been marketable, he continued to declare that he was bisexual.

"In America there's this odd premise," he told me, "that sex is the only measure of morality and that lust in the hearts of our leaders should loom larger as a campaign issue than foreign policy and inflation."

"Even some people who agree with you about sex and politics," I said, "see you as insulting and always making cruel remarks."

"I don't attack people personally," he protested. "I attack their ideas and behavior." This was a crucial distinction in his mind, and he insisted that he chose his targets with care, deflating the pompous, unmasking the fraudulent, and condemning high-placed criminals. He didn't go after defenseless prey. And often he was accused of being cruel when he meant to be funny. In other instances, "I'm being candid, and honesty isn't a quality greatly admired by book-chat writers. So many of them are caught up in a frenzy of mutual back-scratching. I'm not."

A phone on the table beside him rang, and Rat erupted into a yapping furball. The phone had a row of buttons. Gore pressed the blinking one and spoke to a reporter seeking his reaction to a Supreme Court decision that had gone against the novelist Gwen Davis. She had been successfully sued for libel by a doctor who charged that she had based an unlikable fictional character on him.

Gore warned that the decision would have "a chilling effect" on novelists. If the precedent stood, "it'll be a nightmare. They'll have to vet every book for libel. Does this rule out all satire?" He talked slowly, separating his words into syllables, pausing at commas, stopping at periods. He had a horror of being misquoted.

The reporter pressed him to explain how this position squared with his own libel suit against Truman Capote.

"That's a different matter," Gore said. "You simply cannot tell lies about a living person and get away with it."

The litigation against Capote was provoked by an interview in *Playgirl* magazine. Asked why Vidal hated the Kennedys, Capote replied that it went back to November 1961, when Gore had insulted Jackie's mother at a White House gala. Bobby Kennedy overheard this, and he, along with several other men, according to Capote's account, "just picked Gore up and carried him to the door and threw him out into Pennsylvania Avenue."

Bad blood had long been brewing between Vidal and Capote. Both men were combative, both had access to the press and to TV talk shows, and the weapon of choice for both was barbed quotes. In the wake of the sweeping success of *In Cold Blood*, Gore remarked that Capote had "raised lying to an art—a minor art," and added that his career "belongs less to the history of literature than the history of public relations."

By the mid-1970s, Capote had disintegrated into a pill-addled drunk, a pathetic creature who couldn't help but remind Vidal of Tennessee Williams. Vidal was inclined to ignore the story in *Playgirl*. But when it kept cropping up in other venues, in Europe as well as the States, he filed suit against the author and *Playgirl*, demanding damages of one million dollars, plus his legal fees.

Playgirl capitulated after Capote's own witnesses failed to corroborate his testimony during pretrial depositions. The magazine issued a retraction, and Gore dropped his suit against it and offered Capote a settlement. In exchange for fifty thousand dollars—forty thousand dollars of this to pay his legal costs—he would withdraw his libel claim. But Capote refused to settle, and there now seemed no alternative to a ruinously expensive trial that Capote couldn't afford and had no chance of winning.

While Gore was on the phone with one reporter, a different button on the console blinked. He blurted a hasty goodbye and answered the new caller. I didn't mind the interruptions. I figured they reduced the chances of the interview degenerating into a succession of quips and epigrams. But as soon as he hung up, I asked if Gore had read Norman Mailer's *The Executioner's Song,* and his voice fell into quotable cadences. "No. Life is too short and Mailer is too long."

Then the doorbell rang, and Gore rushed to open up for a package delivery. No sooner had he settled back in beside Rat than the doorbell rang again. The deliveryman needed directions to the Valley. Patiently, with no trace of asperity, Gore told him the shortest route.

When we resumed, I brought up a humorous essay he had written about E. Howard Hunt, the Watergate burglar who pursued a sideline as a mystery novelist. To Gore's consternation, Hunt had won a Guggenheim the same year he had been rejected for a grant. "Ever reapply for a Guggenheim?" I asked.

"Never." He snorted in derision. "What kind of money's involved—fifteen thousand dollars? That wouldn't pay the gardener's salary in Ravello. No, I've never won any literary award, and today I don't believe there's one I would accept.

"For years I was nominated for membership in the National Institute of Arts and Letters. Friends tipped me off that I had been blackballed. Finally, in 1976, I was invited to become a member. I sent a telegram: 'The Institute does itself a belated honor. My congratulations. Unfortunately, I cannot accept the invitation. I already belong to Diners Club.'"

This astringency, this belligerent self-sufficiency, might have been necessary early in his career. But even after he achieved riches and renown, he gave the impression of being perpetually embattled. Maybe it galvanized him; maybe the struggle produced better work. Still, I wondered how much it cost him to keep fighting against enemies real and imagined.

"Why do you push yourself so hard?" I asked again. "Do you feel guilty when you're not working?"

"Of course I do," he said with no echo of irony. "After all, I am a puritan moralist."

Suddenly I had a title for my piece, "Gore Vidal, Puritan Moralist." In it, I praised his tireless industry, downplayed his reputation as a social butterfly, and emphasized his seriousness of purpose even in comic works. At the heart of his fiction, I argued, there was a paradox. In his determination to infuse his novels with the same ethical concerns that informed his nonfiction, he sometimes went astray. Where his essays succeeded in being stylishly amusing and at the same time informative, his weaker novels were too explanatory, too didactic. Impatient with the novelist's task of proceeding by implication, Gore jostled the reader along by the elbow, instructing rather than dramatizing, depending on adverbs and adjectives to choreograph the response he desired.

Yet at his best, I concluded, he embedded his ideas in the dynamic interplay of characters and created works of exceptional imagination, wit, and intelligence. In reasonable circumstances he would have been recognized as an author and cultural commentator of singular importance. Instead, he was best known as an opinionated talk show guest.

Otherwise faithful to the transcript of the interview, I confess that I tinkered with one of Vidal's quotations. When he said about *The Executioner's Song*, "Life is short and Mailer is too long," I added, "I take that back. Mailer is short, too."

I dispatched the article to Los Angeles, and days later Gore called and told me to turn to the page, to the very quotation, I had fiddled with. Rather than upbraid me for sticking words in his mouth, he said, "After 'Mailer is short, too,' let's insert 'Isn't it ironic that our would-be most masculine writer has come to resemble—in appearance, if not art—Colette?'"

He took exception to some of my comments about his fiction—he contended that he was a masterful deployer of adjectives and adverbs—but he didn't pressure me to soften my criticism. He did, however, object that I had made one factual error.

"You wrote, 'His hairline has receded a bit.' That's wrong. My hairline has never changed. Don't take my word for it. Look at old photographs. You'll see I'm right. You promised to correct factual errors, didn't you?"

After consulting snapshots on the backs of his early books, I wasn't persuaded and so left the passage as it stood. Then I sent

the piece to *The New York Times Magazine*, along with a letter to
Ed Klein, the assigning editor. Because the *Vidal v. Capote* libel case
was still pending, I explained that I had done due diligence and interviewed Capote's agent/lawyer, allowing him fair comment about
legal issues, and I had let Gore read the manuscript to ensure the
accuracy of his quotations.

Ed Klein phoned and informed me that *The New York Times*
was obliged to pass on the profile. The newspaper had an ironclad
rule against sources reading stories prior to publication.

"You never told me that," I said.

"I didn't think I needed to."

"There was nothing about it in the contract. Don't you normally check with sources and read back their quotes? Are you sure
you're not rejecting it because it's positive about him?"

Klein swore there was no hidden agenda. My faulty profession-
alism made the rejection automatic. The piece was dead, and there
was nothing to be done about it. Full stop.

Nothing, that is, except tell Gore that I had flubbed the assignment. After the botched article about Italy and the imbroglio over
the Graham Greene piece, this was another humiliating setback.
Worse than that, I regretted confirming Gore's paranoia about *The
New York Times*.

To my astonishment, he reacted with equanimity, as if his
worldview had been validated. "I told you *The New York Times* would
never publish a favorable article about me."

"It's not their fault. It's mine. I should never have shown it
to you."

"Don't be ridiculous. Do you think they don't let Kissinger or
Carter or Hollywood stars read what they're going to print?"

(He might have had a point. As recently as May 25, 2013, the
New York Times public editor, Margaret Sullivan, chastised the *Times*
for its history of allowing sources to approve quotations. Even after this policy officially changed, the *Times* permitted reporters to

speak to sources on background and later negotiate with them which quotations made it into print.)

In the end, Gore sighed, not without sympathy, and repeated his pet aphorism. "No good deed goes long unpunished."

Surprisingly, my punishment didn't include banishment from the pages of *The New York Times*. For decades I continued to write for the *Book Review* and *The Sophisticated Traveler*. But I declined to work for the *Magazine*, refusing to do a profile of William Styron when *Sophie's Choice* came out or to interview the king of Afghanistan, whose exile marooned him in Rome. My article on Vidal eventually appeared in the now-defunct *Washington Star*, in *The London Magazine*, and in the *Daily American* in Rome. While Gore offered no value judgment himself, he relayed word that his half sister Nini regarded it as her favorite profile of him.

This set a precedent for his response to all my writing. He never acknowledged reading it, much less deigned to commend or condemn it. At most he mentioned someone else's opinion, usually Howard's, as in "Your new novel, Howard tells me, is hilarious." Or "Howard saw your article about Italo Calvino in the L.A. *Times* and said it's excellent."

But he badgered me endlessly about his hair. The next time I was in Rome, he marched me into the guest bathroom and confronted me with a framed photograph above the toilet. It showed him as a teenager in an army uniform. "The hairline has never changed," he insisted.

In 2003, when Louisiana State University Press published my memoir *Do I Owe You Something?*, the cover was a composite portrait of me, a mosaic made up of shards from different authors I had known. James Dickey's ear, one eye from William Styron, and another eye from Robert Penn Warren formed a jigsaw puzzle face that was capped by Gore Vidal's hair. I gave Gore a copy of the book, and while I wasn't surprised when he said nothing about its subject matter, I waited in vain for him to recognize his own hair.

Months after *The New York Times* aborted my article, the daily book critic Michiko Kakutani interviewed Vidal. Who knows why either of them bothered. Maybe Gore was determined to exact retribution. Maybe Kakutani was unaware of his belief that the *Times* had rejected my piece on him as part of an ongoing vendetta. Whatever their reasons, the two of them took out after each other tooth and claw. I felt no small compassion for Kakutani, who couldn't guess the depth of Gore's fury—a fury she exacerbated by noting that he changed chairs three times to make sure that the photographer shot his "good" (her quotation marks) side. "I suppose you'll call me a narcissist," he taunted her. "Well, a narcissist is someone better looking than you."

His conversation, she wrote, was "punctuated by sighs and yawns. He is afflicted, it seems, by a kind of 'spiritual fatigue.'" As if dead set on repeating every negative characterization I had hoped to correct, she described Gore as "glib," "cold," a man of "pervasive cynicism" and "tart disillusion." Displaying "little hope and less charity," he was in her estimation a misanthropic elitist "dismissive of nearly everything." Although I can imagine how unpleasant dealing with Gore might have been, I also understood, as Kakutani did not, why he felt it was futile to try to charm a reporter from *The New York Times*. His beef against the Great Gray Goose had become the origin myth of his career.

Kakutani conceded that "while Mr. Vidal places himself outside and above most everything he observes, he does not exempt himself from the entropy . . . At the age of fifty-five, he says he now thinks about death all the time, and feels he is 'pretty much at the end.'" Not that this elicited a syllable of sympathy from her.

A week after Kakutani's profile, *The New York Times Book Review* published a largely favorable assessment of *Creation* on its front page. Paul Theroux admired Vidal's ambition and said the novel's "cast of characters could not possibly be bolder."

When I congratulated Gore, citing the review as evidence that the *Times* wasn't monolithic in its attitude toward him, he called me *candido*—the Italian term for Candide-like. "Theroux is a smart careerist. He doesn't want to get on the wrong side of me."

In short, he believed that one conspiracy had trumped another. Rather than accept Theroux's enthusiasm as sincere, he interpreted it as literary logrolling, which had won out over what he viewed as the *Times's* everlasting campaign against him. The only satisfaction Gore derived was a grim sense that once again he had seen through everything—everything, that is, except the cage he was constructing around himself, the trap in which praise and obloquy had become interchangeable.

FIVE

By now I was tenured at the University of Texas, a good job in a good town. Austin was a funky place with fine Tex-Mex restaurants, a thriving music scene, and a sizable contingent of the nation's last hippie holdouts. Whenever I tired of the English Department, I had friends at *Texas Monthly* magazine, where I was on the masthead as the book critic.

Still, like the protagonist of Saul Bellow's *Henderson the Rain King*, I heard a single phrase thrum through my brain. *I want, I want . . .* I wanted to be a full-time writer, not a teacher; I wanted a more varied and involving life; I wanted to live in Rome. With the birth of our second son, Marc, in 1980, I grew more restive, and at the age of thirty-seven I jumped ship and jettisoned teaching and tenure and Texas.

At first we returned to the Villa Chiaraviglio, and for the coming years I remained loosely affiliated with the American Academy, sometimes as a visiting writer, sometimes as a renter of office space, frequently a user of the library, always a player on the paradisiacal tennis court set beside a grape arbor in the shade of an Umbrian pine. An astonishing assembly of talent, the fellows at the academy once put on a Christmas play for children, starring the architect James Stirling as Santa, the poet laureate Mark Strand as

Mrs. Claus, and the novelist Mark Helprin as the Wicked Witch of the North. Frank Stella painted the scenery.

Whenever we felt too cloistered on the Gianicolo, we had all of Rome at our feet. We attended exhibitions in Renaissance palazzi, alfresco movies in the Circo Massimo, classical concerts and even gospel music in baroque basilicas. From time to time there were events at the Villa Medici, where the venerated and widely whispered-about artist Balthus was the director of the French Academy. A skeletal, epicene gentleman, he gave the blasé impression that all the naked nymphets he had painted were no more to him than geometric abstractions.

During the spring of 1981, we squeezed into a tiny cottage emblazoned with a skull and crossbones and a sign that read "Danger of Death," as if that were its ancestral name, like Brideshead or Fontainebleau. Across the street Joseph Brodsky lived in smaller and humbler quarters, a converted garage. Every evening a stream of beautiful women with Eastern European accents rang our bell and asked, "Joseph Brodsky here?" Sean, then six years old, shouted over the intercom, "No, Joseph Brodsky over there." But our propinquity to the future Nobel Prize winner was curtailed when I was nearly electrocuted in the bathtub. Realizing the cottage rested atop a power grid, we moved out.

Linda and I always assumed we would return to the States. Extemporizing from year to year, subletting apartments off the books, we never bothered about rental contracts, visas, or resident permits. Like a lot of foreigners in Rome—like Gore and Howard—we lived in legal limbo, our tax status irregular, our attitude as devil-may-care as any Italian's.

We didn't even own the dented, rust-bucket VW Derby we drove. It belonged to an art professor at the University of California who returned to Rome less and less often until he finally forgot about the car. Occasionally, an indolent traffic cop roused himself to ask about our out-of-date Dutch license plates, but we claimed to be en route back to Amsterdam, and that always got us off.

This life of finagling and subterfuge didn't much appeal to Linda. In spasms of panic, she complained that she felt our identity eroding. Like those jumpy tourists we saw slapping at their pockets to check that their wallets and credit cards were safe, she groped for the security of a fixed point. But I believed that our helter-skelter existence kept me adrenalized and supplied a bottomless reservoir of stories and aphorisms, such as our cleaning girl's mantra "Only for death is there no solution."

Each morning while Linda dropped Sean at preschool—he already spoke *romanaccio* like a native—I propped Marc on a pillow in front of my desk where he watched me work, uttering the odd gurgle. Outside, on Via Angelo Masina wind-driven sycamore leaves scampered over asphalt. Toward midday, Fiats pulled in on Via Giacomo Medici (dubbed "Jack 'Em Off Medici" by academy wags), and lovers plastered the windows with newspapers and set the small cars rocking with their lunch-hour assignations. When Marc started to fuss, I quit working, changed his diaper, and fed him.

My mundane routine could not have been more remote from my fiction. Inspired by that call from *The New York Times* three years earlier, I was writing a novel about a freelance journalist who signs a contract to produce an inside account of life in a Red Brigades cell. Just as the publisher doesn't realize that he plans to fake his adventures in the terrorist underground, the reporter doesn't realize that the plot he concocts mirrors precisely the Red Brigades' plan to kidnap Aldo Moro.

Meanwhile, my first book of nonfiction, *Life for Death*, had come out in the States, and Quinn Martin optioned the film rights and hired a Rome-based screenwriter, Steve Geller, to do the script. Geller and his wife, Joan, became good friends of ours, and we introduced them to Gore and Howard, who lived two blocks away from the Gellers' apartment in Palazzo Cenci.

In addition to his writing—he's best known for his award-winning screenplay of *Slaughterhouse-Five*—Steve played the drums and often accompanied his teenage daughter, Polly, who was a gifted singer. Howard made it a trio and enlivened many an evening with his impersonations of Mel Tormé and Tony Bennett.

As the rest of us enjoyed the sweet life, Gore increasingly seemed glum and off-kilter. When Joseph Blotner, a former professor of mine at the University of Virginia, passed through town, Gore invited us over for a drink. Joe had been William Faulkner's authorized biographer and would also go on to write a biography of Robert Penn Warren. Gore greeted him sourly: "I hope you're not here to Blotner me. Every time you do a biography, the writer dies. I don't care to be Blotnered."

Death was more and more on his mind as he approached the age of sixty, and a parallax yawned between his handsome, haughty persona and the paunchy, disconsolate man he was turning into. At restaurants he no longer ate salads and swiped food off other people's plates. He ordered whatever he wanted, gobbled it down, and asked for seconds. When he got fat, he said that he didn't care. No more dieting, no more workouts at the gym, no more spa retreats and fasting before he embarked on another promotional tour. Once vilified as vain, he was now caricatured as bloated and slovenly, and he swore he didn't care about that either.

In addition to great quantities of wine, he consumed Rabelaisian amounts of scotch and vodka. The old cautionary lectures about hard liquor, and his disdain for contemporaries whose careers had been wrecked by alcohol, no longer played any part in his repertoire. When warned that with his high blood pressure he had better cut back on drinking, he said that he would rather die.

This uncaring mindset eventually colored his work and his behavior. Where once he had been a witheringly funny iconoclast, he now seemed a kind of transgressive performance artist determined to give offense. Delivering the commencement address at

St. Stephen's School, he admonished the young graduates *not* to go forth and multiply. Because there were already too many where they came from, he encouraged them to have plenty of sex, but to dissociate it from procreation.

Previously discreet, he repeated, "I have never had much interest in the sexual lives of real people." Now, like one of those lewd chatterboxes who delight in shocking captive audiences, he often appeared to be interested in little else.

Gore introduced me to his half sister Nini Auchincloss Steers Straight, a slim, dark, attractive woman then in her early forties. Having inherited her mother's good looks and prickly disposition, Nini was rumored to have a strained relationship with Gore. Yet she remained primly attentive as he announced that women in his family all had tight vaginas and narrow birth canals. Later, in his memoir *Palimpsest*, Gore would reveal to readers that Nini had been a virgin on her wedding night, and despite a girlhood spent "astride horses, she had been obliged to undergo last-minute minor surgery."

Smiling prettily, Nini said nothing to contradict her half brother as he launched into a colorful account of his descent from his mother's womb down the birth canal. He described it as a smothering trauma, the cause of his lifelong claustrophobia. "I barely made it out alive."

Gore was also gabby about his father's genitalia. Eugene senior had been born with three testicles. On the other hand, Nini's father, Hugh D. Auchincloss, had the standard two, but as Gore claimed, he had trouble achieving an erection—or so his mother confided in him. His mother's third husband had had only one testicle, and this prompted her to remark after his death that she would never marry again. She could count and knew what came after three, two, one.

Gore hailed from a long line of "over-sharers." His maternal grandmother complained to him that she would never have had children if rats hadn't gnawed through her douche bag. As for his mother, she told him that on her wedding night when she "lost her virginity she wet the bed, which she always felt cast a pall over the marriage."

While professing in public to disdain sexual gossip, Vidal continued in private to embroider stories that he would recycle in bowdlerized form in his memoirs. Long before the scene in *Palimpsest* of Jackie Kennedy demonstrating to her stepsister Nini how to douche after intercourse, Gore informed friends that he was neither puzzled nor appalled by the former first lady's marriage to Aristotle Onassis. Money made the match bearable for Jackie, who, according to Gore, didn't much care for sex. It mattered little to her whether a dreamboat like JFK or a toad like Onassis shared her bed.

A connoisseur of cocks, Gore liked to liven up dinner parties by discussing a fellow who had balls the size and color of eggplants. Then there was the friend whose foreskin resembled a doily. He had it on good authority, he said, from an army medic that although blacks might appear to have larger penises in a detumescent state, they weren't much different from white penises when erect.

Gore's great specialty was celebrity equipment. Reviewing Edmund Wilson's *Thirties*, he noted that Wilson characterized his penis as a "large pink prong." Gore mused, "Surely, Anaïs Nin said it was 'short and puce'—or was that Henry Miller's thumb?"

He described watching Marlon Brando in the locker room at the New York Athletic Club. While Brando's cock was nothing memorable, Gore said that even in his prime Brando had a huge flabby ass and wore a corset. Peter O'Toole, by contrast, was emaciated everyplace except for his sex. Dennis Hopper, he said, had an attractive tuft of hair above his buttocks.

According to Gore and Howard, their good friend Paul Newman was priapic. Staying erect long after he climaxed, "he just keeps sawing away," Howard said. "And exhausting Joanne," Gore added.

Eventually, Gore lost all reluctance to hold forth on his own sexual performance. He conceded that the only true thing Truman Capote ever said was that Gore Vidal was a lousy lay. "Capote could not have known at first hand . . . [but] I did think it a good tactic in my youth to spread the word that I did nothing at all in bed to please others—on the ground that unwanted seducers would pass one by. It's not the worst tactic, by the way, though hardly foolproof, as fools found out."

By his account, he had sucked only one cock to orgasm, that of a sailor named Tiger. When challenged about his bisexuality and asked when he had last had intercourse with a woman, he mischievously recalled an orgy "when I plugged into the wrong socket." He never understood the mania of heterosexual couples for prolonging sex. "I just want to get on and get off as quickly as possible. Then get it up and come again."

His preferred position—at any rate the one he most often spoke about—was "belly rubbing," by which he meant standing or lying face-to-face with a man and creating friction to the point of climax. Women he had had sex with as an adolescent, he said, avoided pregnancy by letting a man insert his penis between their buttocks—without penetration, he stressed.

Yet for all his coruscating chatter about sex, Gore struck me as one of the least sensuous, least tactile men I ever met. Despite a drawling, relaxed voice, he was physically rigid, coiled. Like any politician, he had a good handshake. But he shrank from human contact otherwise. Once in a crowded car, Linda sat on his lap and said afterward she could feel him freeze. Whenever he danced, he looked like a windup toy. In his essay "Pornography" he wrote that an "effort must be made to bring what we think about sex and what we say about sex and what we do about sex into some kind of realistic relationship." In his own life, however, he never appeared to come close to achieving that harmony.

One evening Gore arrived alone at our apartment for dinner with a cast on his foot. He had injured it in a fall, he explained, and was limping badly.

Among the guests was Andrea Lee, a *New Yorker* writer whose first novel, *Sarah Phillips*, would come out in 1984. Gore and she had the same publisher, Random House, Lee gushed, and the same editor, Jason Epstein. "He really loves me, and he really loves my book."

"Oh, I bet he does." At the moment Gore would not have said that Epstein loved him. Their friendship was foundering on Gore's insistence on producing idiosyncratic comic novels that alternated with his historical blockbusters. His new one, *Duluth*, dealt with an imaginary city that drifted from place to place and whose inhabitants might love it or loathe it but could never leave it. Gore protested that his money-spinning bestsellers gave him the right to such experiments. He was sick of the formulaic requirements of historical fiction and welcomed the rejuvenation he derived from these jeux d'esprit.

As Lee cataloged the prepublication indicators that she believed augured well for her novel, Gore interrupted. "Has anyone noticed that as a man gets older his wee-wee begins to grow back into his body?"

Lee subsided into baffled silence.

"When I stepped out of the shower this morning," Gore said, "I looked at myself in the mirror and noticed that my wee-wee is growing back into my body."

Lee reacted in all earnestness as if this might be a question that she should submit to *The New Yorker*'s famed fact-checkers. "Don't you think your body is, you know, gaining weight and growing down around your penis so it just looks like it's growing back into you?"

"No, it's definitely retreating. I remember Cecil Beaton making a similar observation when he was my age. He asked Greta Garbo and me, 'Has either of you noticed as you get older your sexual organs get smaller?' And Greta said"—Gore lowered his voice in imitation of Garbo's—"'Would that I had that problem.'"

Another night, we invited an American couple to dinner with Vidal. Avid readers, arts patrons, and opera and concert lovers, they declared that of all the historical figures they admired, Abraham Lincoln held a place of prominence. Having read Gore's novel about the sixteenth president, they were eager to quiz him.

Over drinks, they behaved like country clubbers schmoozing with the head pro the night before the member-guest golf tournament. They were giddy and starstruck, but no matter how ditzy their questions, Gore remained cordial and never condescending. Then, as we moved to the table and Linda was ladling up the soup course, he said, "Do you mind if I ask a question?"

The couple urged him to go right ahead.

"What do gals think about anal intercourse?"

I concentrated very hard on the tortellini spinning in my bowl of *brodo*.

Linda said, "You know, Gore, gals don't talk about anal intercourse."

"Oh, come on, they're doing it."

"They may be doing it. But they don't talk about it. Not on the first course, they don't."

If I maintain that my fortieth birthday party is remembered by millions, I'm not indulging in mythomania. Most of the guests might have forgotten it, and no one else in the world would have been aware of it, had Pat Conroy not transmuted the event, as he has other raw material from his life, into fiction.

Pat pitched up in Rome in 1981, a refugee from Atlanta, Georgia, with a new wife, Lenore, and three children—two from her first marriage, one from his. They knew nothing about Italy—not the language, not a single street of the city—and Lenore was pregnant. She gave birth at Salvator Mundi Hospital, a block from our apartment, and Linda and I became their daughter Susannah's godparents.

Most writers are cannibals, but Pat Conroy is exceptionally voracious, and despite his slow, shambling country-boy demeanor, he's quick on the uptake. Soon after we met, the two of us made a trip to Munich for Oktoberfest and talked in the car for twelve hours. When Pat later showed me a draft of *The Prince of Tides*, it contained an anecdote lifted intact from one of my monologues about a Marine Corps friend of mine who confessed to killing a little boy during the Korean War to save his own life. It didn't matter to Pat that I had already used the scene in my novel *The Toll*. He adapted it to his purposes, substituting World War II for the Korean War.

Subsequently, in *Beach Music*, Pat returned to our road trip to Munich and pinched another yarn, this one about a scrawny kid from my high school who surprised everybody by standing up to a bully on the football team. He didn't do so empty-handed. He was carrying an ax handle, and when the bully taunted him, "You don't have the guts to use that," the boy bashed him in the head, fracturing his skull and knocking out several teeth. Letting his imagination run riot, Pat changed the ax handle to a baseball bat.

In no way do I condemn Pat. Stories, as the ancient Greeks advised, belong to those who can tell them—or at least to those who hear them and put them on paper for the largest audience. For the record, however, Conroy's fictionalization in *Beach Music* of my fortieth birthday party begs correction. He described it as a glittering Roman gala at the palazzo of a rich, glamorous American couple, Paris and Linda Shaw. Conroy's protagonist, Jack McCall, dresses for the festivities in a tuxedo. Pat himself wore his habitual outfit—plaid flannel shirt, rumpled khakis, and jogging shoes. McCall brings along his beloved daughter, Leah, whose beauty and intelligence impress none other than Gore Vidal, the great man doing a star turn as a character under his own name. "This child is lovely," says the fictional Vidal. "She looks as though she were born in pearls."

In truth, the party transpired in our drafty, threadbare apartment. Far from a *salone* festooned with gilt-framed art, the living room was decorated by forty origami birds that Sean had folded and strung from the ceiling. Linda baked a cake large enough for the requisite number of candles and several dozen guests, among them Peter Schweitzer, the new CBS bureau chief, and Dennis Redmont, the head of the AP, who gave me a ceramic coffee mug fired in the succulent shape of Gina Lollobrigida's torso. Mickey Knox, never one to show up empty-handed, arrived with the actors Eli Wallach and Anne Jackson.

When I introduced Gore to Conroy, he didn't marvel over Pat's daughter. Susannah was at home with a babysitter, fast asleep. Instead, he expressed admiration for Pat's second novel, *The Lords of Discipline*; the military academy setting reminded him of West Point. "I'd have liked it more," he added, "if you had been honest about the book's real theme."

"What's that?" Pat asked.

"Those boys were a bunch of masochists and sadists. You can bet they were having sex together in the dorm."

Conroy did a comic double take, like Li'l Abner flummoxed again by Daisy Mae. "They were?"

"It couldn't be clearer that the narrator and his best friend were banging each other."

"This is going to come as a great shock to Pig," Pat said of his roommate at the Citadel who, like so many real-life characters, played roles in the novel.

Gore later mused that he had pondered Conroy's mass popularity. "He's onto something. He's tapped into a truth the rest of us never knew ran so deep in the United States. His novels about dysfunctional families indicate just how fucked-up our nuclear units have become."

Gore had remarked that Dorothy Parker frequently contracted a bad case of the "frankies" when she drank too much. At which point she cut loose with whatever was on her liquor-soaked brain. Perhaps alcohol explained his own growing penchant for ignoring nuance and pronouncing opinions that a man of his acumen should have recognized would prompt a backlash.

In print and in interviews he staked out a position on Israel that sparked accusations of anti-Semitism. When he defended himself, drawing the distinction that he was against Zionism, not Jews—after all, he lived with a Jew—this didn't satisfy his detractors. Soon he was under attack not just by literary critics but by Op-Ed authors and TV talking heads. Rather than respond in a measured fashion—better yet, apologize for any misunderstanding—he became more strident. In conversation, he started referring to Israelis as "desert gods" and joked that "whom the gods would destroy they first put hair on their backs."

He swore that he relished the combat, and he never neglected an opportunity to debate. But there began to be symptoms of battle fatigue. Hollow-eyed one instant, he turned irascible the next. He complained that he couldn't sleep no matter how much he drank. Then, admitting to more than physical exhaustion, he lamented that he was tired of living and wanted to die. This unnerved Howard, who, in his agitation, sometimes told Gore to quit talking about it and go ahead and drop dead.

Over the 1984 Christmas holidays, Don and Luisa Stewart hosted a party at their apartment on Via Margutta. A former artist's loft, with one wall of windows and two opposing walls paneled in mirrors, the immense living room accommodated a tall spruce tree and the whole Roman throng, plus William Gaddis and Muriel Oxenberg and Gay and Nan Talese.

A resident writer that year at the American Academy, Gaddis had been scheduled to give a public reading from his work, reputedly the first of his career. Perched in an armchair, dressed like a banker in a gray suit and rep tie, he scolded the crowd, saying he had failed to find a single copy of his novels in the library or in any bookstore in the city. "I can only assume nobody is interested in my fiction. So I'll be reading to you from Gogol's *Dead Souls.*"

I guess we should have been grateful that he didn't read it in Russian.

Talese was in Italy researching a memoir about his family's roots. This was in the aftermath of the scandal over *Thy Neighbor's Wife*, the chronicle of his adventures on the sexual frontier. He and I had played tennis at the academy court, and as we warmed up, he shouted, "This is what I love most in life—this and fucking." Behind us echoed the sound of scholars banging shut the windows of their studios.

This might make Talese sound like a buffoon. Actually, he was focused, disciplined, and exact. In his hotel room he kept an intricate outline of his new book pinned to the wall. Next to the phone lay a list of numbers and names, each spelled out phonetically, along with a chart indicating the current dollar value of various denominations in lire.

That night at the Christmas party Gore loitered with me next to one of the iron columns that supported the loft's high roof. He admitted that he was steering clear of Talese, who had been heard to carp that Gore sucked all the air out of a room. "So I stand here," he said, "occupying as little space and consuming as little oxygen as possible."

He and Howard were due to depart soon for their annual excursion to Bangkok, "in our relentless pursuit of AIDS." He hadn't caught the disease yet, he told me, because "as the Bible says, it's better to be a giver than a receiver." This irreverence about "the gay plague" that was then incurable and killing tens of thousands of men and women worldwide didn't endear him to activists who tried in vain to get him involved in the campaign to discover a cure. As he flippantly retorted, "I'm not a doctor or a scientist." In part this was perfectly consistent with his deep-seated thanatophobia, which had even kept him away from his beloved grandfather's funeral. But it also reflected his aversion to being categorized as gay. His refusal to embrace a uniform sexual identity sometimes sounded close to self-loathing. He acknowledged asking a Thai lady-boy how he could bear doing what he did. "He claimed he liked it," Gore said. "But who would like blowing an old man?"

Downcast that night, he expressed regret for all he had left un- done in life. A failed campaign in the 1982 California Democratic senatorial primary had killed off his last political aspirations, he said. He would never again pursue elective office.

I assured him that he wielded more influence and enjoyed greater freedom to speak out on issues as an author than he would have had as a politician. How could he conceive of trading his life in Italy for the fishbowl of Washington, D.C.? He'd lose whatever privacy he had managed to preserve.

"If you're speaking about sex," he said, "I would have led a secret life, no different from plenty of American pols. The problem isn't sex. I should have run sooner. If I had, I'd be a senior senator by now, probably with a wife and a couple of kids. Maybe I'd be president."

I conceded that I had more difficulty picturing him as a father than as president. He said, "I have a daughter. At least I think I do."

This was another tune he had taken to strumming, and it drove Howard to distraction as surely as Gore's plaint about longing to die. Sometimes he seemed certain about this daughter and discussed her mother and the man who had raised the kid never realizing he wasn't the father. At other times, the child sounded as speculative and implausible as his unrealized presidential ambitions.

It occurred to me that Gore was mulling over a counter-life, much as had Philip Roth and Paul Theroux in their novels. John Cheever, by contrast, had lived his alternate narrative. After a long marriage and three children and suburban conformity, he swerved into the gay side of his psyche. Gore appeared to be doing the opposite—considering the heterosexual possibilities of his character.

But whatever else he might have become, it defied reason to envision Gore as an electable candidate. His sexuality was the least of his drawbacks. Never a glad-hander or baby kisser, much less an ass kisser, he wasn't the kind to beg for cash. A documentary, *Gore Vidal: The Man Who Said No*, showed him at a fund-raiser in an ocean-side mansion in California. Prefacing his speech, he quipped that it was a pleasure to be in the People's Republic of Pacific Palisades. That got a laugh. It's doubtful it filled his campaign coffers.

More crucially, his political platform violated middle-of-the-road American values. And there were financial shenanigans he would have been hard put to explain away—his dodgy tax status in Italy, his announcement during the Vietnam War that he had, supposedly in protest, exchanged all his dollars for deutsche marks. "Civic virtue," he wisecracked, "can be remarkably profitable." Already a dubious figure for spending most of his adult life abroad, he had secret bank accounts that, if revealed, would have caused scandal. Worse, he had considered relinquishing U.S. citizenship and becoming Swiss or Irish, both to avoid taxes and to register his disgust over Vietnam. Right-wingers, even liberal Democrats, would have eviscerated him.

His political instincts, it struck me, had always been undermined by an antinomian aspect of his personality. The same might be said of the conflict in his literary achievement and his failure to choose between fact-based fiction and sometimes ingenious, sometimes goofy "inventions." Call it a surfeit of talent or a radically contradictory nature. Or give it the Greek name hubris. In the end, his cravings often canceled each other out.

When he started in again about wanting to die, I wondered whether this might be another bit of role-playing. But if so, he stayed in character for the next thirty years. I told him I hated hearing him sound so depressed.

"What do you care?" he asked with a touch of belligerence.

"I like you. I don't want you to die."

"I don't believe that. You're like all young writers. You can't wait for the old ones to die off so you can replace them."

"Whether you're dead or alive, I don't see me replacing you. I'm strictly mid-list."

He couldn't be jollied out of his bleak mood. "Maybe you don't want me out of the way. But Edmund White, I bet he'd like to see me gone."

"I don't know about that. Call me selfish. I'd rather you stick around as long as you can."

"It won't be long."

"Are you thinking about killing yourself?"

"No. I'll just keep leading my life." He raised his glass in a wry toast. "This'll take care of things soon enough."

Less afraid of sounding fatuous than of not making an effort, I found myself attempting to convince him how much he mattered to people. But at that moment his writing, his money and fame, his friends, the admiration of millions of readers, his status as a sort of international ambassador without portfolio, a man unafraid to speak truth to power, meant nothing to him. He had led a life of vaulting ambition, and by any objective standard he had succeeded. But now it seemed as if nothing he had accomplished was, or could ever be, enough.

SIX

If Gore was to be believed and alcohol was his suicide weapon of choice, it was worth wondering whether he drank because he was unhappy or whether he was unhappy because he drank. Most likely a psychiatrist would have speculated that it was a bit of both and diagnosed him as a depressed self-medicator who drugged his symptoms rather than address the underlying causes.

Gore would have rejected any such analysis. For him, psychotherapy fell into the same category as voodoo shamanism. Long ago, Anaïs Nin had suggested he needed treatment, theorizing that he was frozen in childhood and that his arthritic knee, the result of frostbite in Alaska, was a symbol as blatant as Achilles' heel. Gore dismissed this as ridiculous. He claimed that he didn't have an unconscious mind. Everything about him was right on the surface. So what was a shrink supposed to dig up?

As a young man, however, unhappy at the failure of a love affair, Gore had sought out therapy, and although he abandoned the couch after a few sessions, he never entirely abandoned the quest for the key to his psyche. In *Palimpsest*, he agreed with the Belgian mystery writer Georges Simenon that "a novelist's work is not an occupation like another—it implies renunciation, it is a vocation, if not a curse, or a disease . . . It is sometimes said that a typical novelist is a man who was deprived of motherly love . . . The fact is that the need to create other people, the compulsion to draw out of oneself a crowd of different characters, could hardly arise in a man who is otherwise happy and harmoniously adjusted to his own little world. Why should he so obstinately attempt to live other people's lives, if he himself were secure and without revolt?"

It required no great penetrative powers to tease out the implications here and apply them to Gore and his manipulative, alcoholic, sexually promiscuous mother, who, when not ignoring him, mercilessly mocked him for his failures and who, when he became a success, protested that she was responsible for his accomplishments. Alienated at an early age, he elevated alienation to a personal aesthetic and seized every opportunity to prove that he couldn't be hurt by people—indeed could scarcely be touched by them and didn't need them as anything except an audience. He acted as if the only thing that mattered was not whether he was loved but whether his ideas and especially his books were revered.

That this egocentric attitude might prompt, in a Newtonian fashion, an opposite and equal reaction never appeared to have occurred to him. When reviewers, voters, or literary rivals pushed back against his imperiousness, he didn't modify his behavior. He raised the stakes, displaying an arrogance bordering on pugnacity that not only made him enemies but often made him miserable. Which, in turn, made him drink and offend more people, who responded by withholding the acceptance he yearned for.

Over the years I witnessed rebuffs, some quite petty, that utterly unraveled his Olympian self-possession. When Mark Phillips, a CBS correspondent, transferred from Russia to Rome, I wanted him and his British wife, Sue, to meet Gore, and we arranged to have dinner at Settimio all'Arancio. He and Howard had recently returned from an antinuclear conference in Moscow, one of Mikhail Gorbachev's liberalizing overtures during the glasnost period. As we waited for a table and for Sue, Gore delivered a lecture on the

Soviet Union, describing it to Mark as a Third World nation with a First World arsenal. "It's Upper Volta with ICBM rockets. It's never been a real threat to the West. That's U.S. cold war propaganda. Typical scaremongering."

Sue showed up at the end of this disquisition and took exception to it. A correspondent for CBC TV in Canada, she believed her two years in Russia gave her a better grasp of the situation than Gore's brief junket.

"Who are you?" he demanded.

"Who are *you*?" Sue shot back.

Gore's riposte? There was none, not in words. He whirled around and stormed from the trattoria with Howard tagging along behind him.

This might be dismissed as no more than the pouting of a prima donna. But it indicated how, for all his pretense of detachment, Gore seethed just beneath the surface with infantile rage. Moreover, it suggested that his lifelong ambition to become president was far from matched by the stable makeup required of a national leader.

The next morning, Howard called and blurted, "Who was that British cunt?"

"All this," I said, "because she didn't recognize Gore."

"Oh, she recognized him, all right."

"So you're saying Gore's insulted because she disagreed with him?"

"He's insulted because she's a cunt." Having done his duty as Gore's defender, Howard hung up.

When William Styron, bedeviled by his own demons of depression and drunkenness, visited Italy in 1982 with his wife, Rose, and spent a few days in Ravello, the setting of his third novel, *Set This House on Fire*, Gore invited him for a meal at La Rondinaia. Styron was impressed by the villa's opulence. But back in Rome he disparaged Vidal's wealth. "Fags," Styron said, "don't have kids to support and college tuition to pay."

To which Gore acidly replied, "Yes, and fags don't get to marry department store heiresses."

On notice that his feelings were far tenderer than I had ever realized, I proceeded cautiously when the American Academy asked me to invite him to appear at a fund-raiser. In every respect he was the right choice, one whose links with the academy went back decades to the days when he did research there for his novel *Julian*. In the end he agreed to speak as long as it was understood that he wouldn't produce anything original for the occasion. He would read an essay, soon to be published in the States, about the American political situation. Then he would answer—or "entertain"—questions from the audience.

That left the matter of a dinner party the academy proposed to throw for him. The director drew up a guest list that included Linda and me; that year's Prix de Rome writing fellow, Mark Helprin, and his wife, Lisa; and a septuagenarian female classicist to balance the table with Gore. I pointed out that unless I was mistaken, Gore would prefer to sit with his partner, Howard Austen.

"You mean Vidal's gay?" the director asked.

"I believe he would say bisexual." It struck me as wise to add that Helprin was adamantly opposed to Vidal. An affable guy under most circumstances, he used to do push-ups with Sean and Marc on his shoulders. One summer he had lived in our apartment, and not content to leave it spotlessly clean, he had obsessively cataloged all my books by size. When I offered to introduce him to Gore, Helprin refused. A conservative who went on to write speeches for the Republican candidate Bob Dole during the 1996 presidential campaign, he objected to Vidal's stance on social and sexual issues, and as an American who held an Israeli passport and bragged of serving in the Israeli military, he considered Gore an anti-Semite.

(Years later, when Donald Barthelme was at the American Academy, he, too, declined to meet Gore. His refusal had nothing to do with politics, sexual or otherwise. He didn't appreciate Gore's lampooning his work in the essay "American Plastic: The Matter of Fiction.")

Gore's talk attracted one of the largest audiences in the academy's history—so large it spilled out of the auditorium at Villa Aurelia and into adjoining rooms where spectators clustered around a closed-circuit TV. The academy would have been smart to charge admission. That surely would have raised more money than his puckish appeal for contributions. "I was in the library the other day and noticed it needs repairs. Rats were eating the codexes. Write a check and stop the rot."

Afterward, as the crowd pushed forward with books to be signed, a slender Italian with a high, brainy forehead and a slightly supercilious manner ask me to introduce him to Signor Vidal. I recognized Italo Calvino, whom I had interviewed for *The Washington Post* after he moved back to Italy from Paris and settled in Rome, several blocks away from Gore's apartment. Calvino told me he wanted to pay his respects to the author who had introduced his work to an American audience with an essay in *The New York Review of Books*.

Delighted to meet Calvino, Gore posed for a photograph with the man he referred to as Il Maestro. The snapshot would appear in his biography erroneously dated nine years earlier, in 1974, the date of Vidal's essay on Calvino. This mistake might have indicated magical thinking on Gore's part, an expression of how deeply he wished their friendship had lasted longer. Il Maestro died in 1985, a few short years after their first meeting.

When Gore realized that Calvino hadn't been included in the academy dinner, he was perturbed, and his perturbation deepened as he learned that an openly gay couple had been invited as replacements for Mark Helprin and his wife. He later complained to me about being stereotyped. Did the academy imagine he couldn't cope with straight people or that they couldn't abide him?

Then, too, the gay couple was campy and swish, and Gore fumed, "One either likes men or one likes women. I like men. Not something in between."

"Not Anna May Wong and consort," Howard said.

Thus an event that should have been a confirmation of his popularity and importance ended up being perceived by him as an affront.

In the October 1985 issue of *Architectural Digest*, Gore wrote that he woke up one morning to discover that he had spent three decades in Rome. His best explanation of this was to quote Howard Hughes, who, after huddling for years in a darkened hotel room, his hair down to his shoulders, his fingernails grown to six-inch claws, said, "I just sort of drifted into it." But the "drift" in Vidal's case was doubly perplexing because Italy isolated him from his muse, which as he wrote in *Screening History* wasn't a person—it was American movies, his original and enduring love.

Of course, Italy didn't lack its own intermittently brilliant film industry. But Gore never had much interest in foreign movies or in art house fare. He was a creature—and a creator—of Hollywood films, and among his favorites were *Being There* with Peter Sellers and *Saturday Night Fever* with John Travolta. The former tickled his funny bone, the latter his libido.

Movie houses in Rome showcased current hits from the States dubbed in Italian, and for Gore, never fully fluent in the language, this was a torment. Even for perfectly bilingual viewers, watching a dubbed film was often frustrating or gut-splittingly funny, depending upon one's POV. No matter how well the dialogue was synchronized with the actors' lips, there remained the difficulty, especially with American slang, of deafness to the right accent and intonation. Gangsters, whether from the East Coast or the West, from the Sunbelt or the inner city, were dizzily dubbed into Sicilian dialect. Blacks, whether street-smart, dirt-road dumb, or Uncle Tom middle-class, sounded Calabrese. And businessmen, be they Wall Street venture capitalists or Houston hog belly hustlers, came across as bourgeois Milanese, pronouncing their *r*'s like Elmer Fudd.

The substance of dialogue also risked getting lost in translation. The dubbed version of Sam Shepard's *Fool for Love*, for instance, set off giggles when a crusty cowpoke asked his girl to fix him cappuccino and a *cornetto* for breakfast.

The lone Roman theater that featured *versione originale* American films was the Pasquino. A shabby establishment in Trastevere located between a lesbian bar and a deconsecrated church, it was frigid in winter, stifling in summer, and malodorous year-round. On its cracked plastic seats a clutch of bums slept off their hangovers. The projectionist sometimes seemed to be asleep, too, and ran the reels out of order.

While the Pasquino was the low road, there was for select souls a yellow-brick high road, a veritable stairway to heaven. The American ambassador Maxwell Rabb and his wife, Ruth, were avid movie buffs, and on Sundays they hosted lunch at their residence, the Villa Taverna, then escorted a hundred or so guests—a mixed bag of Italian notables, American businessmen, foreign diplomats, and military officers—to an outbuilding that had been refurbished as a deep-carpeted, wood-paneled screening room. There the lights dimmed, and a first-run American movie, in English no less, flickered to life.

At first, Gore wasn't among the anointed. Neither was I, though not for want of trying. I had a friend at the U.S. embassy, Robert Bentley, who attempted, and failed, to get Linda and me into the Sunday screenings. But when I introduced Bentley to Gore, he had no trouble convincing Ambassador Rabb that Vidal, with his heralded Hollywood connections, had the correct credentials.

A genial couple in their seventies, of the same generation and slightly baffled bonhomie as President Ronald Reagan, the Rabbs were starstruck. Or as some put it less politely, they were starfuckers who tirelessly courted actors and directors and celebrities passing through town. They once persuaded Michael Jackson to forsake his hyperbaric chamber and favor them with his presence at the Villa Taverna. So it wasn't entirely surprising that they overlooked Vidal's rabble-rousing reputation and welcomed him despite his caustically funny review of *Ronnie and Nancy: A Very Special Love Story* and his incessant reference to the president as a shill hired by corporate America to hit his mark and mouth his ghostwritten lines.

What did surprise me was that Gore accepted. I would have expected him to fire off a stinging rebuke as he had when he turned down the National Institute of Arts and Letters. But that was before I sufficiently understood how much emotion Gore invested in honors. Eventually, he changed his mind about the National Institute of Arts and Letters and accepted its renewed offer of membership. And after declaring that he had no interest in literary prizes, he reconsidered when he won the National Book Award for nonfiction.

More amazing still, he and the Rabbs became friends, and when Joanne Woodward flew into Rome without Paul Newman, Gore invited the ambassador and his wife to a dinner in her honor. Unfortunately, this conflicted with the fortieth anniversary of the liberation of Naples, where the ambassador had committed himself to participate in a commemorative ceremony. He couldn't cancel his appearance without causing an international incident.

But sources at the U.S. embassy leaked word that Max Rabb was wavering. He and Ruth agonized over missing an evening with an Academy Award winner. In the end, celebrity prevailed over diplomatic protocol, and the ambassador kissed off Naples and attended the party for Joanne Woodward.

Months later when the White House announced that Nancy Reagan would visit Rome, Ambassador Rabb drew up a roster of

VIPs to be introduced to the first lady at a formal reception. Gore Vidal's name was among the luminaries. As soon as the White House got wind of this, it struck him off the list. Embassy insiders assured me that the decision upset Rabb, but he had no stomach for a fight with Washington. And so Gore once again became persona non grata.

When I spoke to him, it was obvious that Gore was aggrieved, although he tried to spin it as a joke. Having fallen out of favor with the Kennedys, having had a place of pride on Nixon's enemies list, and now being cold-shouldered by the Reagan administration, he drawled that he had scored a hat trick. He wouldn't be drawn into a discussion of Max Rabb's fecklessness, and he didn't reply when I pointed out that people clamored for his company and took advantage of his hospitality. Journalists plagued him for interviews, authors troubled him for blurbs, schools and political groups appealed to him to deliver free lectures. But when the chips were down and he might have appreciated a bit of reciprocity, he was usually deemed, as the British say, "unclubbable."

To my astonishment, the incident did not end Gore's dealings with Max Rabb. He continued to accept invitations to embassy events, just as he continued to welcome the ambassador at his Rome apartment and his villa in Ravello. The access, the status, hard-won and late in coming, meant too much to him.

Whenever I hear Gore Vidal accused of bitchiness, of rude disregard for people's feelings, I remember the slights and gratuitous insults he suffered. And I think about disappointments I didn't learn about until later. A three-person judging panel voted *Lincoln* the winner of the 1985 Pulitzer Prize for fiction. But the Pulitzer committee exercised its authority to override this decision and deny Gore the prize.

Maybe he was right, after all, when he swore that anybody who is not paranoid is not in full possession of the facts.

Gore on the occasion of his becoming an honorary citizen of Ravello in 1983, standing with Italo Calvino on his left and Luigi Barzini and Alberto Arbasino on his right. (Photograph by Joan Geller)

Gore seated between the film producer Deborah Schindler and the casting director Todd Thaler at our apartment in Rome in 1983.

(Photograph by Linda Mewshaw)

Gore at a dinner party in the mid-1980s at our apartment in Rome,
seated next to the Italian-American journalist Anselma dell'Olio.

(Photograph by Christina Nagorski)

Howard Austen in a peacock chair in our apartment in 1985.

(Photograph by Christina Nagorski)

Gore with Daria Stewart. (Photograph by Luisa Stewart)

Gore with Donald and Luisa Stewart in Rome in 2002.

(Photograph by Linda Mewshaw)

Gore with Peter Matthiessen at the 2009 Key West Literary Seminar.

(Photograph by Michael Blades)

Gore's office in 2013. (Photograph by Linda Mewshaw)

The pathway to La Rondinaia, overgrown with wisteria pods, in 2013.

(Photograph by Linda Mewshaw)

SEVEN

In the early 1980s, the modest success of *Life for Death*, my first book of nonfiction, was wiped out by a libel suit. In short order, the film option lapsed and was never renewed. My U.S. royalties were frozen, and the paperback edition was postponed. The British edition, already in page proofs, was delayed pending a resolution of the litigation. Ultimately, the book's U.K. publication was canceled altogether.

In contrast to my stressful and frequently contentious career, Gore Vidal's lofty status, I assumed, armor-plated him against problems that plague less successful authors. But he made it clear that he was well acquainted with contractual squabbles, publishing disputes, and libel suits. Indeed he believed he had earned the equivalent of a Harvard law degree dealing with his legal troubles. He advised me to resign myself to a long siege and to hire my own attorney. "Don't trust your publisher, and remember your agent looks after your sales, not your legal interests. If you're lucky, the case'll never come to trial. It'll be settled out of court."

During the discovery phase of my case the claimant demanded *Life for Death*'s sales figures, and Doubleday produced some stunning numbers. According to its records, the trade edition had sold 6,000 copies. But various book club editions, all of them subsidiaries of Doubleday, had sold 275,000 copies at a greatly reduced royalty, in some cases less than five cents a unit.

"You're getting screwed," Gore said. "You need to hire an accountant as well as a lawyer."

To convince me that Doubleday's figures didn't add up, he did something authors seldom do. He shared his recent royalty statement; *Creation* had sold 90,000 copies in trade and 30,000 as a Book-of-the-Month Club selection. "That's the normal ratio," he said. "Not your absurd numbers. Probably the publisher is distributing copies of the trade edition and accounting them at the book club royalty."

I did as Vidal urged—hired a lawyer and threatened legal action. The dispute with Doubleday dragged on even longer than the libel suit, which was, as Gore predicted, settled out of court. In the end I won some financial satisfaction from my publisher, not enough to make me whole, as lawyers put it, but sufficient to allow me to keep squeaking by in Rome.

Still, I was forced to set aside my novel about the Red Brigades and sign on for another nonfiction book, *Short Circuit*, this one about the men's professional tennis tour. Gore bucked up my spirits, reminding me that he had written TV scripts and pseudonymous mysteries when he was under economic duress. He saw nothing disreputable about sports reporting, and as for tennis he had depicted Jim Willard, the central character in *The City and the Pillar*, as a teaching pro and opened the novel with a hard-fought match between two teenage boys who become lovers. Gore encouraged me to shower with John McEnroe and report to him how the meanest man on the circuit was hung.

For a while it appeared that film work might also help me stay solvent. The British producers of *Chariots of Fire* and *The Killing Fields* wanted an original screenplay based on the 1981 assassination attempt against Pope John Paul II. According to their high concept, the gunman, a disturbed Turk named Ali Acga, was a Soviet

agent, a clever killer for hire, like the posh English gentleman as-
sassin in Frederick Forsyth's *Day of the Jackal*. On the first day of
his trial, however, when Acga faced the world's TV cameras and
proclaimed, "I am Jesus Christ," the Brits decided he was a jackass,
not the Jackal, and dropped the project.

Then Lina Wertmüller, the director of *Swept Away* and other
Italian hits, contacted me. "I haf read your novels, and I luf your dialogues." In stutters and starts, it emerged that she had completed a
script in Neapolitan dialect that had been translated on the cheap
into English to attract foreign investors and an international cast.
While she had succeeded in securing financing and the services of
Harvey Keitel and the Spanish actress Ángela Molina, Wertmüller
feared the script was unshootable as it stood. "Please, read it," she
said, "and I pay you money to tell me is this English or what."

We met at her apartment on Via Principessa Clotilde, where I
hunkered in acute discomfort on a throw pillow. Titled *A Complicated Intrigue of Women, Alleys, and Corpses*, the script fell, I told her,
into the "or what" category. A variation on *Lysistrata*, it portrayed a
coven of women who vow to stamp out the drug industry in Naples
not by withholding sex from dealers but by killing them during intercourse by needling heroin straight into their testicles. This ex-
cruciating premise was made more painful by a translation that read
like Esperanto crossed with Jabberwocky. Because much of the
Neapolitan dialogue consisted of an incessant repetition of the same
four-letter Anglo-Saxon fricative, it might be said that I had been
hired to find synonyms for "fuck."

Compulsively putting on and pulling off her trademark white-
rimmed glasses—dozens of pairs of identical spectacles were stra-
tegically placed around her apartment so that she always had several
close to hand—Wertmüller hovered over my shoulder during the
rewrite, debating every word I substituted for the original smut.
"Screw," "hump," "bang," "pork"—we sounded like schoolkids snick-
ering in the lavatory, reveling in filth. My energy flagged long before

hers did. She relished "bumping the uglies," which I stole from the screenplay of *The Boys in the Band*. When I told her I was kidding, we couldn't possibly use it, we'd be accused of plagiarism, she wouldn't hear of deleting it. The phrase made it into the film's final cut.

We wasted the worst part of a week arguing over two lines. Ángela Molina, meant to be a sympathetic character, has a cute six-year-old son. He races over and leaps onto her lap, and she exclaims, "Oh, fuck my ass, but you're heavy." It took all my powers of persuasion to convince Lina that middle Americans wouldn't accept this as the likely response of a loving mom.

Then we clashed over an exchange between Molina and Harvey Keitel. When she rejects his sexual overtures, Keitel wistfully wonders what Molina ever saw in him. "I loved your pirate's chest," she says, "and you always smelled like seafood."

"What do you mean by pirate's chest?" I asked Lina.

"She loves his *corpo*, his body." She patted her meager *poitrine*. "He has the big chest of a pirate."

"In America a pirate's chest is a box full of gold doubloons. And nobody believes seafood smells nice."

"*Ma senta bene*." She kissed her fingers. "It smells good, seafood."

"Maybe to Italians. Not to Americans."

"This cannot be."

"Look, Lina, you simply have to choose—"

"Shoes?" She changed glasses and glanced at her feet.

"You have to decide whether you're making a movie for a domestic audience or an international one."

"You ruin my dialogues," she cried. Off came the glasses, on came an interchangeable pair, and off we spiraled into other linguistic altercations.

As the rewrite haltingly progressed, Gore inquired whether I had been paid.

"Not yet."

"Let me offer a suggestion. Hold on to the last pages of the script and tell Lina you won't turn them in until you get your money. In cash!"

I did as instructed, staging a sit-down strike on a throw pillow in Wertmüller's living room. She reasoned, she sweet-talked, she threatened, but I hung tough, and she made a phone call. An hour later, a burly man thundered down Via Principessa Clotilde on a motor scooter, and in what might have been a scene from her movie, he forked over a brown paper bag stuffed with thousands of dollars worth of lire.

Helpful as Gore had been, it wasn't unprecedented for an older, accomplished author to extend advice and sympathy to a younger, less exalted one. It was quite a different matter, however, to offer material support. When he heard me lament how hard it was in our cramped apartment, with Sean and Marc underfoot, to finish *Short Circuit*, Gore urged me to work at La Rondinaia. He and Howard were flying to the Far East; I could stay at the villa as long as I liked.

"Drive down with your family and have Thanksgiving dinner with us," he said. "Howard'll show you around, introduce you to the help, and walk you through the shops in the village. After that you're on your own."

Nothing demonstrated more graphically how little Gore resembled the chilly, uncaring misanthrope portrayed by the press. True, he didn't gush with sentiment or declare undying friendship, and when I expressed gratitude, he brushed it off with a sarcastic retort. But I couldn't then—and can't now—imagine Hemingway handing over Finca Vigía outside Havana or Somerset Maugham vacating the Villa La Mauresque on St.-Jean-Cap-Ferrat for an impecunious colleague.

Linda and I and the boys, along with a babysitter hired to keep

Sean from breaking furniture and Marc from falling off a balcony, packed into our borrowed, battered VW and puttered south. From frantic Naples we swept past sleepy Sorrento onto the Amalfi coast. Though the weather was cool, the landscape lent itself to illusions of perpetual summer. Royal purple bougainvillea unscrolled from window ledges, and Virginia creeper vines trellised against walls had turned red as roses. Entire mountainsides were terraced like staircases for giants, with vineyards and citrus and olive groves on each step.

Painted in pastels and rich earth tones—salmon pink and sienna, pumpkin orange and Pompeian red—towns nestled beside tranquil coves. Colonized by Saracens ages ago, the area retained Arabic touches—keyhole arches, variegated tile domes, and labyrinthine streets. Every vest-pocket piazza called to mind a party in the rooms of a sprawling palazzo owned by a loud and lively family that prided itself on hospitality to strangers.

The road to Ravello cut inland and climbed a series of looping hairpin curves. On one side, the Lattari Mountains sheered up out of the Mediterranean to an altitude of 4,700 feet. On the other side, cliffs plunged into the sea. In every direction, the perspective seemed skewed, alternately lengthened and foreshortened, the distances, like the light, dreamily bent. Cars squeezed over to the edge of the asphalt as buses passed by, sometimes emitting a metallic ping as bumpers kissed.

We parked in the main square in front of the duomo and hiked a quarter of a mile along a footpath to a locked gate. Bundled up in a tweed jacket instead of his standard blazer, Vidal escorted us onto his property, along a majestic colonnade of trees. Fallen chestnuts crackled underfoot, their husks as spiny as sea urchins.

His eight acres had staggering views of a cobalt sea speckled with brightly painted fishing boats bobbing beneath a sky of scudding clouds. Far below, automobiles beetling along the corniche looked toylike. Up here, the air was pure and scented with rosemary, lavender, and thyme. "As you can see," Gore said, "my wants are simple."

He recalled his first visit to Ravello in 1948 with Tennessee Williams at the wheel of a secondhand army jeep. It was a tale he had told so often he had his timing down as tight as a borscht belt comedian's shtick. As they careened up the corkscrew road, Tennessee chose that moment to reveal, "I am for all intents and purposes blind in one eye." Between Tennessee's erratic driving and the splendor of the landscape, Gore conceded that he had had "a mixed first impression" of the Amalfi coast. Now it inspired him, he claimed—inspired him to write a film script "to get the pool finished. That's a powerful inspiration. I always date things by which money, which book, built them."

The villa, constructed by Lord Grimthorpe in 1930 for his daughter, clung to a craggy cliff face, defying gravity and graphically incarnating its name—La Rondinaia means the Swallow's Nest. The floor plan, Gore said, replicated a classic Roman house, with rooms opening off long corridors. More accurately, it had the hallmarks of Islamic style—barrel-vaulted ceilings, arched doorways, and windows with filigreed iron grilles. Moroccan carpets covered terracotta floors. The dining room table was a slab of glass balanced on trestles of stone, and around it were ranged ornate chairs whose arms ended in hammered brass rams' heads. Gore had bought the chairs at an antiques shop. "The guy swore they were hundreds of years old. I think they were made at Cinecittà for *Ben-Hur* when I was there writing the script."

Downstairs, where he and Howard had their bedrooms, there was a sauna and a gym with a slant board for sit-ups and racks of barbells for bodybuilding. This corner of the villa had the musty air of a mausoleum. It didn't appear that anyone had exercised here or fired up the sauna for years.

Bookshelves lined a hall that ran the length of the house, and they did show signs of constant use. "Read whatever you like," Gore said, "but put each book back where you found it."

He pointed to wall light switches at knee level. "They were that way when we moved in. The previous owners were so old, maybe they were bent double. Or maybe they were afraid they'd fall down and not be able to reach a light. They come in handy when Howard and I are crawling around drunk in the dark."

The villa's nerve center and real workout room was located in the study. Olive wood burned in a massive tufa fireplace inlaid with tiles. In front of it, a mosaic tabletop duplicated the pattern on the ceramic pulpit in Ravello's duomo. A wooden table served as Gore's desk, and here he had written all his books starting with *Burr*. I anticipated that he would put it off-limits. Instead, he told me to make space for myself among his manuscripts, notes, and mail and write where he did.

The cook at La Rondinaia prepared a passable facsimile of an American Thanksgiving feast, and once Linda and I fed the boys and the babysitter got them to bed, we polished off a pumpkin pie and ice cream and washed it down with local Episcopo wine. Gore discussed his involvement with Naples 99, an organization dedicated to rescuing a city that Italians had written off as the Calcutta of Europe. He called himself "a trombone in an orchestra of encouragement to raise money to restore Santa Chiara, et cetera."

Then he jumped to a mini-lecture about the Amalfi coast, praising it as an excellent perspective from which an American writer could take the measure of his homeland. James Fenimore Cooper had finished *The Last of the Mohicans* in Sorrento, and it amused Gore to picture Cooper setting up shop, just as Vidal had done, on the gulf between the Roman ruins at Pompeii and the Greek ruins at Paestum and spending years chronicling past events in the United States.

There was more, there was much, much more, that he said. Howard didn't wait around to hear it all. He went to bed. Then

Linda begged off. Finally, when I couldn't hold my eyes open any longer, I offered Gore a hand to climb off the floor, where he reclined like a Roman emperor. He chided me for abandoning him and declared that he was comfortable right where he was.

For all I know, he spent the night there. In the morning he woke up before I did, and by the time I had eaten breakfast, he and Howard were packed and ready to depart for Bangkok. They surrendered the keys to the house, lugged their suitcases to the main square, and caught a cab to the Naples airport.

Days later, Linda, the boys, and the babysitter left in the VW Derby, and I stayed on alone. Alone except for the man who laid a fire each morning in the study, the maid who cooked my meals, the team of gardeners that tended the grounds, raking up baskets of fallen chestnuts. As I got down to business, I anticipated an easy run of writing on a coast where authors as different as Norman Douglas, D. H. Lawrence, William Styron, Graham Greene, and Gore Vidal had created art while living in what amounted to works of art.

What I hadn't counted on was how damned uncomfortable such living can be. Wind whistled through the loose windows at La Rondinaia, billowing the curtains and chilling the tile floors. The fireplace wheezed and gave off feeble warmth and weak light. By midafternoon I was freezing and wrapped up in a blanket at Gore's desk as I drudged away at my manuscript. It rained without cease for two weeks. As storm clouds trailing what looked like a Medusa's tentacles raked in off the Mediterranean, La Rondinaia trembled on its foundations and threatened to slide down the cliff face. Several nights the telephone and the electricity went on the fritz, and I had to read by candlelight, like Abe Lincoln roughing it in a log cabin.

The cook swore that the villa was haunted, and each evening before dark, she hastened toward the gate flashing her first and little fingers against the evil eye. The other employees followed her, while I rattled around in the cold rooms, wary of bumping into ghosts.

It came to me that despite its luxurious appointments and spectacular views, the villa was no berth for sissies or sybarites. It was a purpose-built factory dedicated to hard labor. Maybe during summer it was different. Maybe then Sting, one or two Rolling Stones, Bruce Springsteen, and Susan Sarandon and Tim Robbins rollicked in the gardens. Even so, I'm convinced Gore lived here mainly to work, wake up in the morning, and work some more.

Evidence of this was on shelves all around me in his novels and essay collections. As I reread his early books, I became conscious of the modesty of his fledgling efforts and the evolving quality of his prose. The home-spun declarative sentences in *Williwaw* and *The City and the Pillar* had gradually given way to the supple timbre of his later high-plumed style. It was rare for any writer, particularly one who had enjoyed early commercial and critical success, to develop an altogether different degree of mastery, to keep reaching for the next rung on the ladder.

I felt I could do no less than try to follow his example. I stayed on task. I stayed at his desk and kept working until I finished my book. That, after all, was the point of the place and of Gore's lending it to me.

In September 1983, Linda and I returned to Ravello when the town conferred honorary citizenship on Vidal. Friends flew in from as far away as Los Angeles to celebrate the occasion and mingle with Italian dignitaries. Marella Agnelli and a triumvirate of writers—Luigi Barzini, Alberto Arbasino, and Italo Calvino—were in attendance, and there was grandiloquent speechifying, followed by Neapolitan singing and fireworks, and windy panegyrics to the town, one by Gore, extolling "this earthly heaven, this Ravello, of blue sky and sea, gray limestone and olive."

The overarching vibe of the evening was one of extemporized wackiness. Gore maintained in his memoir that Italo Calvino had arrived at the ceremony uninvited and volunteered to speak off the cuff. But earlier, in a reminiscence for *The New York Review of Books*, he had claimed that the town fathers of Ravello had invited Calvino to participate in the ceremony. Having written an introduction to *Duluth*, describing Vidal as "a master of that new form which is taking shape in world literature and which we may call the hyper-novel or the novel elevated to the square or to the cube," Il Maestro now unburdened himself of another vatic pronouncement: "I must ask myself if we are indeed in Ravello, or in a Ravello reconstructed in a Hollywood studio, with an actor playing Gore Vidal, or if we are in the TV documentary on Vidal in Ravello . . . or whether we are here on the Amalfi coast on a festive occasion, but one in 1840, when, at the end of another Vidal novel, *Burr*, the narrator learns that the most controversial of America's Founding Fathers, Aaron Burr, was his father. Or since there is a spaceship in *Duluth* manned by centipedes who can take on any appearance, even becoming dead ringers for U.S. political figures, perhaps we could be aboard that spaceship, which has left Duluth for Ravello, and the ETs aboard could have taken on the appearance of the American writer we are here to celebrate."

Among the guests I spotted no ETs or centipedes. But there were the Hollywood producers Doug Wick and Lucy Fisher, the redoubtable Mickey Knox, the AP bureau chief Dennis Redmont and his wife, Manuela, the screenwriter Steve Geller and his wife, Joan, and Frederick "Freckie" Vreeland, a CIA agent at the U.S. embassy and son of the *Vogue* editor Diana Vreeland. By sheer happenstance *Gentlemen's Quarterly* was doing a photo shoot on the Amalfi coast, and George Armstrong enlisted a team of tanned, muscular male models to add an erotic touch to the party.

More eye-catching, in my opinion, was the long-limbed, mocha-colored woman who made an entrance in a floor-length gown with a silver lamé bodice and a back cut low to the cleavage of her buttocks. Like the boys in Versace and Armani suits, she appeared to be a model—as fine boned and elegant as the high-fashion mannequin Iman, straight out of Africa and onto the catwalk.

Once Gore's official investiture was finished, guests processed back to La Rondinaia. Gliding along the cypress allée at a stately pace, the silver-gowned woman stayed tantalizingly ahead of me. Then, as we reached the villa, I got stuck with Italo Calvino and lost track of her. No insult to Il Maestro, but since that evening at the American Academy, I had seen him on several occasions, and he was an ultraserious sort and not nearly as attractive as the black swan. Still, I admired his work and told him how much I had enjoyed *Invisible Cities.*

Accustomed to compliments from far more authoritative sources, Calvino gave no discernible reaction to mine. The two of us stood, drinks in hand, at a balustrade that teetered above a blue abyss of sky and sea. In a cream-colored jacket and white tie, he might have been a figurine on a wedding cake. As Gore escorted Calvino's wife, Chichita, inside to show her a photograph of Montgomery Clift, Il Maestro gazed in the general direction they had gone.

"Your evocation of place was beyond compare," I nattered on, wishing I were in one of the invisible cities he had so vividly evoked.

"Do you read Calvino in Italian," he asked, "or in translation?"

It was the only time I have ever heard an author refer to himself in the third person. "Translation," I confessed.

"Then you have never read Calvino." With that he, too, flounced off to admire Montgomery Clift's photograph.

Put in my humble place, I watched one of the bronzed *GQ* hunks lead Linda onto the dance floor for a slow number. Howard nudged me. "Hey, don't get mad. Get even. Lemme introduce you to somebody that's dying to meet you."

Lazily supine on a chaise longue, the black beauty peered at me through eyelids at sleepy half-mast. Howard referred to her as

Egitta. No last name. Graceful as an egret, she rose to her feet. I'm six one. She was a good two inches taller, and when she pressed close to dance, her pelvis hit me in the solar plexus.

"Where are you from?" I asked in Italian.

"I live in Rome," she answered in English with an accent I couldn't place.

"Where'd you learn to speak English?"

"Arkansas."

"You're from Arkansas?"

"You got something against the South?"

"Nothing at all. I mistook you for an Ethiopian princess. Are you married?"

"Yeah, to that teeny-weeny Italian over there with the beard. But don't let that bother you."

"Any kids?"

She threw her head back in a throaty laugh. "I babysat my brothers and sisters. That's enough kids for me. How about you?"

"Two boys."

"Hey, macho man! Ever feel like trying something on the side?"

"Like what?"

Again, the throaty laugh punctuated by a pelvic thrust. I was torn between the desire to get away from Egitta and the desire to go away with her.

"Are you a model?" I asked.

"No, I'm in the movies." Then, after a gravid pause, "Porno."

As I was about to ask soft core or hard, Manuela Redmont rushed over and shouted, "Did they get it all?"

Hands on canted hips, Egitta cooled her heels, waiting for the next dance.

"Well, did they?" Manuela demanded.

"Get what?" I said.

"They keep cutting off his cock. But it keeps growing back."

Suddenly I saw Egitta, as they say, through new eyes and noticed what had escaped me before—the size 12 shoes, the snow-shovel hands, the Adam's apple and five o'clock shadow. It seemed that everyone at La Rondinaia except me recognized her as a transsexual star of stage, screen, and TV. With no notion of the etiquette on these occasions, I thanked Egitta for the dance and hastened to mix myself a drink.

At the bar, Steve Geller and Mickey Knox were arguing about a yellow-and-black checkered sport jacket that Freckie Vreeland had draped over the back of a chair. They concurred that it was the most appalling item of men's apparel they had ever seen. But Geller wanted to wear it as a joke and Mickey wanted to throw it away. Mickey won and hurled it off the terrace. We all watched as it soared like an unmanned hang glider past orchards and vineyard stakes, over fences, and farther on down the mountainside toward the sea. And as it fell, things fell from its pockets—coins, keys, pens, and pills—so that it lost weight and sailed on and on. The sight of that airborne coat headed for an inevitable crash landing left me wondering whether Egitta had blundered into the party. Or was she Gore's honored guest, the reincarnation of—perhaps even the inspiration for—*Myra Breckinridge*?

Later, when I raised this question, Gore told me Egitta wasn't the only transsexual he had known. He described an encounter with one who, as intimacy impended, sloshed baby oil between her legs. "That was the giveaway," he said. "No matter how ingenious the surgeon, only God can create a self-lubricating vagina."

EIGHT

Although the festivities in Ravello had provided some diversion, Gore's mood remained flat to frighteningly low. With alarming frequency, he declared that he was sick of living and wanted to die. Then, continuing his slow-motion suicide, he went back to the bottle.

His editor Jason Epstein was of the opinion that he had never known anybody who drank more than Vidal, but he insisted that he had never seen him drunk. I, on the other hand, had watched Gore stagger through the streets of Rome and sink to his knees stepping off curbs. In Ravello, I had held my breath along with the crowd at the bar Al San Domingo and winced as he splatted to the pavement. This humiliated Howard, who stalked off, letting his partner struggle to his feet alone.

Deepening Gore's melancholy, Tennessee Williams had choked to death in 1983 on a plastic bottle cap, presumably while drunk. "All his life he was afraid of suffocating," Gore told me. "That that's how he died must have been unbearable." He acted out the last minutes of the Glorious Bird's life, pantomiming his gnawing at the plastic bottle and fatally inhaling the cap. Gore clawed at his neck as he imagined Tennessee must have done. "Ghastly," he said. "Ghastly."

Drinking didn't just feed Vidal's depression. It ravaged him physically, bloating him with forty or fifty pounds of fat. Though he argued otherwise, his hangovers had to have been horrendous. He did acknowledge that he wasn't feeling well, but he blamed the nuclear meltdown at Chernobyl in Ukraine. When newspapers reported that a radioactive cloud had spread over Rome, Gore, with his rich history of hypochondria, had a ready-made excuse for his ailments. They were all due to toxic fallout, whose severity, he charged, had been suppressed by conspiratorial governments and craven journalists.

Meanwhile, his beloved Rat contracted cancer of the mouth but managed to survive for a few years thanks to Gore and Howard's extravagant care. While touched by this show of devotion, guests chez Vidal were less than charmed as Rat's tumor started to suppurate. But Gore cuddled the dog close to him in his chair and seemed to regard its drawn-out death throes as a test of who his true friends were.

Despite the vile smell and bloody discharge, celebrities kept coming to his dinner parties. Norman Jewison, Carroll O'Connor, and Murray Kempton graced the table, the film director discussing politics instead of show business, the actor shedding his identity as Archie Bunker and proving himself every bit as liberal and issue oriented as the journalist Kempton. Whatever else was on the menu during those evenings, avid debate about national and international affairs was a mainstay.

Usually, Gore postponed his bleating until after the A-list guests departed. Then, morphing from a brilliant pundit into a pitiable creature, he groused that he suffered from a drastically reduced sex drive. Again he drew no connection between alcohol and his troubled libido. Again he theorized that radiation from Chernobyl had deadened his desire. Or perhaps it was boredom, he said, and the inevitable consequences of advancing age.

Mickey Knox, born four years before Vidal, was of the school that believed the older the buck, the harder the horn. He boasted that he had no sexual problems.

Gore scoffed at him. "Don't tell me you can still get it up. I need real technicians now, not street trade."

Howard didn't look any healthier than Vidal. He, too, had gained weight, and because he was shorter, he had a harder time hiding the extra pounds. After a bout of cosmetic surgery in the States, the two of them returned to Rome looking like mummies, skin stretched tight across their cheeks, reddish wads of scar tissue bunched behind their ears. Even after they revisited the surgeon for some post-op tidying up, Howard appeared haggard. Despite his emphysema, he wouldn't quit smoking, and his torch singing at parties was curtailed now by paroxysms of coughing. Gore lamented that La Rondinaia sounded like the TB sanitarium in Thomas Mann's *The Magic Mountain*. Then, when Howard began forgetting to bring in the mail, he wisecracked that they resided at Villa Altaheimer.

For a man as death haunted as Vidal, his decision to appoint an authorized biographer seemed wildly out of character. Nothing figured to leave him more mindful of his mortality than counting down to the conclusion of what was, in effect, an extended obituary. But Norman Mailer had commissioned a biography while he remained in what passed for ruddy good health, and William Styron had done the same. The practice struck some as an all-too-blatant attempt to shape their critical legacy, an impulse Vidal couldn't deny that he shared.

More perplexing than Gore's permitting a biographer to paw through his private life—this after protesting that he had done nothing that deserved close examination—was his choice of the *Newsweek* book reviewer Walter Clemons as his Boswell. He had always expressed contempt for what he called "book-chat" writers. He also vilified the hacks of academe, but I would have predicted that he would pick an eminent scholar, one who had produced a generous appraisal of an author whom Gore admired.

Instead, he settled for an affable journeyman who had never written a biography and hadn't published a book in two decades. After launching his career in fiction and winning the Prix de Rome in 1962, Clemons had fallen victim to writer's block. According to colleagues at *Newsweek*, he had difficulty meeting deadlines for short magazine pieces, much less for longer projects. Still, Vidal professed to be satisfied.

To be sure, Clemons was satisfied. He had landed a $350,000 advance from Little, Brown, prompting Jason Epstein, who fell short in the bidding, to taunt Gore, "You've led a very expensive life."

As Walter Clemons discovered, Gore had also led a complicated and largely unknown life populated by fascinating characters. Flying to Rome, Clemons set about interviewing people whom Gore socialized with and depended upon much more than he did the boldfaced names linked to him in gossip columns. It wasn't long, however, before Clemons departed for other venues, and Gore crabbed that his authorized biographer viewed research as an opportunity to lark around Hollywood, London, New York, and Washington, rubbing elbows with his betters. He accused Clemons of dithering and sarcastically observed, "I've seriously handicapped him because I've never had a breakdown, divorce, [or] autistic child."

These disclaimers couldn't disguise the fact that while he might have avoided certain conventional domestic discords, he showed increasing signs of emotional fragility and rage. *The New York Review of Books*, formerly an unflinching ally, had, in Gore's opinion, begun to betray him. He railed that the magazine rejected anything he wrote that offended readers whom "Bob Silvers [the editor] might climb socially."

His relationship with Jason Epstein also continued to deteriorate—in part, no doubt, because of large unearned advances—and he found himself fighting a series of losing battles with Random House. I assumed he would do as Graham Greene told me he had done when Viking pressured him to retitle *Travels with My Aunt*. Greene shot off a telegram: "Easier to change publishers than title." Instead, Gore stuck with Random House even after it only grudgingly agreed to publish *Live from Golgotha* and at first refused to bring out *United States: Essays, 1952–1992*. The consensus was that at more than a thousand pages the collection was too expensive and unwieldy to print. In the end, Random House offered what it might have believed was a deal-breaking contract that called for no advance against royalties. Gore capitulated. That *United States* went on to win the 1993 National Book Award was some consolation, but it didn't assuage his anger.

One night Linda and I arrived at the penthouse on Largo Argentina for a small dinner party—just Howard and Gore and the Academy Award–winning actor Walter Matthau and his wife, Carol. Rather than his uniform of blue blazer and gray trousers, Gore sported a guayabera, a loose-fitting Latin American shirt that couldn't conceal his huge paunch. Too fat to fasten his trousers, he wore a pair of suspenders in place of a belt.

Carol Matthau, a handsomely groomed woman, could not have presented a more vivid contrast to Gore or to her grumpily humorous, hound-dog-faced husband. Dainty and petite in a white knit dress, she resembled a porcelain doll, an impression heightened by bleached-blond hair the consistency of cotton candy and a pale complexion dusted with chalk-white powder.

A great beauty in her day, the stepdaughter of a Bendix Corporation executive, she grew up in an eighteen-room apartment on Fifth Avenue, attended the Dalton School, and was friends with Gloria Vanderbilt and Charlie Chaplin's future wife Oona O'Neill. Yet even as a demure debutante, Carol had had a wild streak. In her teens, she met the playwright William Saroyan, a man twice her age, and married him. Indeed she married him twice—the first time for six years, the second time for six months. According to her memoir, *Among the Porcupines*, the marriage ended definitively when Saroyan flung her down a flight of stairs and choked her in front of their children.

She had a droll, self-mocking style and remarked in her memoir, "It seems strange that everyone I'm writing about was very famous . . . Didn't I ever find anyone interesting who was not famous? Actually, no, I didn't."

Before marrying Matthau, she had been courted by the British critic Kenneth Tynan and the American author James Agee. For a time, Truman Capote had been Carol's close confidant, and he had partly modeled Holly Golightly in *Breakfast at Tiffany's* after her. Their relationship foundered, however, when Capote published a couple of indiscreet, unflattering excerpts from *Answered Prayers*, his unfinished magnum opus, which divulged intimate conversations with Carol and her friends.

That night in Rome, Capote served as ripe conversational fodder. Gore's suit against him had been settled in 1983, with Capote apologizing in writing, denying that he had ever intended to "cast aspersions upon your character or behavior." He pledged he wouldn't speak about Vidal in the future.

Less than a year later, Capote died at the home of Johnny Carson's ex-wife Joanne, cueing Gore to respond that for the sake of fair play he now felt duty-bound to die in Johnny's house. He flippantly characterized Capote's death as "a good career move," a line he cribbed from postmortems about Elvis Presley predicting that the singer's passing would spark a renaissance in his record sales.

In a letter to Paul Bowles, Gore wrote a more measured assessment of Capote's afterlife prospects. He "will now be the most famous American writer of the last half of the 20th century. No one will ever read a book of his again but no one who can read will be able to avoid the thousands of books his life will inspire. Since he has told the most extraordinary lies about every famous person of our time, the hacks will have a field day recording the sorts of lies *they* usually make up. T's affair with Camus, T's help getting Marilyn [Monroe] aborted, T's blow job of President Kennedy . . . Well, he is what this vulgar tinny age requires. RIP."

At dinner with the Matthaus, after several bottles of wine, Gore fetched a cut-glass decanter of scotch and drank most of it himself.

"Don't bother pouring it into a glass," Howard said. "Just swill it right out of the bottle."

Gore ignored him, lurched to his feet, and lunged toward a sideboard for yet another bottle. His suspenders snapped, and one of the clips shot out from under the guayabera like the Alien from a victim's chest. His trousers slid down his pale legs, puddling at his shoes.

"There he is, ladies and gentlemen," Howard announced. "Gore Vidal—elegant, patrician, and to the manor born."

Gore flopped back in his chair, pulled up his trousers, and resumed drinking. While Walter and Carol Matthau and Linda and I sat mute, Howard said, "For his next trick he'll stand on his head and whistle Dixie."

In the space of time I had known him, Gore had become the kind of novelist he used to blister with disdain. Having mocked Faulkner, Hemingway, and Fitzgerald as rummies and lampooned his contemporaries—Mailer, Williams, and Capote—as lushes who squandered their talent, having described Irwin Shaw and James Jones in their last years on Long Island as looking like "a couple of mangy old lions," he was now as bad as any of them, and nobody except Howard dared tell him to take a look in the mirror.

Linda's parents visited Italy just once in the decade and a half we lived there. My father-in-law, Robert E. Kirby, the retired CEO of Westinghouse, served on several corporate boards and had flown to Europe for meetings. A Republican, a keen golfer, and a craggily handsome man, he was on the PGA board and appeared in a number of TV commercials promoting the game. Indeed, he dressed like a golf pro, in white loafers and white belt, green jacket and pastel trousers.

Steve and Joan Geller threw a dinner party at the Palazzo Cenci for Bob and his wife, Babs, and I suffered heart-stopping anxiety when they invited Gore and Howard. What if Gore's suspenders snapped and his trousers dropped to his shoe tops? What if he asked my in-laws their opinion of anal intercourse?

Linda assured me her mother would enjoy the evening. An avid TV fan—the Kirbys had thirteen Westinghouse television sets scattered about their Pittsburgh home—Babs felt on a first-name basis with Gore Vidal after watching him so often on the Carson and Cavett shows.

In his customary blue blazer and gray slacks, not a guayabera, Gore made no wisecracks about Bob's bird-of-paradise plumage. The two alpha males took to each other as fellow top people. While my father-in-law, whom I had never known to read a novel, waxed dithyrambic about Vidal's work, Gore couldn't have been more complimentary about Westinghouse's washing machines and lightbulbs.

"Glad you like them," Bob said, adding, "These days we make most of our profits off big-ticket items, like nuclear power and desalinization plants."

"Not to mention TV and radio stations," Gore chipped in. "That's where I got my start in TV, on *Studio One*. I'd have starved if Westinghouse hadn't sponsored a new play every Monday night."

Gore recounted how those live telecasts in the 1950s posed extra challenges. With no retakes and limited time for rehearsals, every miscue was witnessed by millions. "Remember the refrigerator that wouldn't open?" he asked.

This was the kind of glitch that didn't normally set well with Bob Kirby. Partial to everything that bore a Westinghouse logo, he preferred to believe that none of his products had ever had a defect. But Gore doubled him over with laughter as he recalled an incident that made front-page news in the United States and that Gore later repeated word for word in *Palimpsest*: "In a dramatically—even reverently—lit corner of the studio theater there was a special chapel for the Westinghouse refrigerator, for which we toiled. The high priestess–saleswoman Betty Furness was absent that evening, and her place had been taken by a young actress, who briskly described the virtues of the refrigerator. 'And it all works so easily. You just *press* the *magic* button . . .' She pressed the button. Nothing happened. Close shot of actress's panicky face. Then, as she gabbled incoherently, the sound of a crowbar prying open the door. On cue now, she turned, pressed the button and, like a lover come home from who knows what crusade, the door fell into her waiting arms."

Gore's performance, carried off with aplomb in front of a potentially antagonistic audience, charmed the Kirbys. And the next morning he phoned Linda to say, "I loved your father. He was a bore, but he was my kind of bore. I grew up around plenty of worse men than him."

Grateful that the evening had ended without incident, Linda didn't much mind that he added, "He's cute as a bug's ear, but let me let you in on a little secret. Your father has known male flesh."

Prone to identify everybody as gay, sapphic, or bi, Gore suspected his own father of having "known male flesh" as a result of a schoolboy crush that paralleled the plot of *The City and the Pillar*. What's more, he conjectured that this alleged affair had been immortalized in a novel by Robert McAlmon. A minor literary figure in Paris in the 1920s, McAlmon had grown up in Madison, South Dakota, Eugene Vidal Sr.'s hometown, and in an autobiographical narrative, *Village: As It Happened Through a Fifteen Year Period*, he described an ambiguous adolescent, simultaneously attracted to and antagonistic toward a handsome star athlete named Gene Collins, who was bound for West Point.

Whether Eugene senior and McAlmon ever had sex together,

no one could possibly know now. But an aunt once confided to Gore, "Well, it's pretty clear he [McAlmon] liked Gene too much." And that was all the proof he needed—that and the fact that McAlmon had "fingered Hemingway as a fellow fag, to Hemingway's fury."

Rome, which purports to be eternal, may seem to be trapped in amber, but it's actually in a state of constant flux. Some changes occur with the inexorability of one earth plate grinding against another; nothing registers for centuries until the ground cracks and new contours emerge. Other changes transpire in a matter of months: grand palazzi metamorphose into luxury hotels; churches become supper clubs. Still other changes take place from one hour to the next: a market folds its stalls and is supplanted by a parking lot; a famous fountain turns into a car wash.

So it shouldn't have shocked me when I felt the cobblestones shift under my feet. Although I liked to imagine myself blissfully married to Rome, the union had never been one of calm conjugal joy and drowsy domesticity. The city was a demanding mistress whose erotic allure existed in precarious equipoise with a penchant for brutal tantrums. Something as prosaic as mailing a package or cashing a check could devour a whole day and ignite hysterical shouting matches.

Then, too, what had been a cheap sweet life in the 1970s turned costly as the 1980s advanced toward the 1990s. The apartment that used to cost us two hundred dollars a month now rented for fifteen hundred. And the pollution that was eating at the city's marmoreal splendors ate into our lungs. Marc came down with allergies that required him to hook up several hours a day to an inhaler and strap on a breathing apparatus that resembled an astronaut's helmet.

Still we stayed on, reckoning the advantages against the disadvantages. Who, we reasoned, would be so foolish as to forsake a life blessed with so much art, history, fine wine, and delicious food? What novelist in his right mind would relinquish the trove of stories that Italy supplied with the same spendthrift abundance as it produced flowers in every season, music for every emotion, and salty wisdom for every frustration?

We stayed on even after many of our friends—Pat Conroy, Steve Geller, Bob Katz—left Rome. We stayed on after the Guardia di Finanza, Italy's fiscal police, commenced cracking down on expat tax dodgers. Suddenly there was a stampede toward the exit, and many U.S. television and newspaper bureaus shut their doors, one step ahead of the law. Even Gore wobbled, confessing to me that he had paid a $100,000 bribe to bury a tax squabble with the Italians.

As the struggle to remain in Rome stretched on and on, Linda wondered whether we were doing a disservice to Sean and Marc by raising them abroad. While she and I could return to the States and reintegrate, she worried that the boys might end up stranded in a twilight zone between Europe and America, not quite comfortable in either place, foreigners wherever they went. Unless we relocated soon, she envisioned them as adults in New York or Los Angeles behaving like the bumbling tourists we poked fun at in Rome—bewildered by the currency, unable to operate a pay phone, reluctant to use colloquialisms for fear of uttering some unspeakable barbarity.

And so in 1989 we abandoned Italy. Yet no sooner had we left than I regretted it. Rome-sick, plagued by memories, I dreamed of the dozen different apartments we had rented, the views from different terraces, the Tiber seen from different bridges, the ceilings I had gazed up at as I prowled the streets at night, dazzled by gold scrollwork, candlelit vaults, murals of angels and saints. Soon I was inventing excuses to fly back. I shot off article proposals and depended on magazines and newspapers to pick up my plane fare. With every arrival, I checked in with Gore, as if he were a customs official who had to certify my reentry, and he always teased me, "What learned journal sent you this time?"

For anybody who bothered to keep track, I suppose my publications in *Gourmet* and *Granta*, *Sports Illustrated* and *The Sophisticated Traveler*, *Playboy* and *The Chronicle of Higher Education* did seem slightly schizophrenic.

In 1990, half a dozen years after its publication, *Year of the Gun*, my novel about the Red Brigades, was made into a movie at Cinecittà. Hired as a consultant, I hadn't a clue what that entailed. So before meeting the director, John Frankenheimer, I spent a few hours with Gore, who told me, "You're here to agree with everybody and stay out of the way."

"But they asked me to read the script."

"Tell them what they want to hear. It's terrific. Then take your money and go home."

Of course, I couldn't keep my mouth shut. I complained to Frankenheimer that while the screenwriter hadn't retained a single line of my dialogue, he had stuffed into the character's mouths expository passages from the novel that were absurd as conversation. Frankenheimer nodded, kept his counsel, and, on the evidence of the finished film, never passed along my comments to the lead actors, Sharon Stone and Andrew McCarthy.

He did, however, allow that he was familiar with *Short Circuit*, my book about pro tennis. Once a highly ranked junior, he had played on the team at Williams College and, now a robust sixty-year-old, he traveled with his own teaching pro. Did I care for a match?

The match he had in mind pitted the two of us against his teaching pro, a terrific player named Harold Hecht who had starred at Cal-Berkeley. When Frankenheimer and I eked out a 6–4 win, I guessed that Harold had thrown the last two games—a smart move for a fellow who aspired to a film career. But Frankenheimer was as exultant as if he had won Wimbledon.

That night Gore informed me that Harold was the son of the

famed producer Hal Hecht, Burt Lancaster's partner in one of Hollywood's first successful independent production companies. Gore wanted to meet him, and when we got together for a meal at Da Fortunato, he whispered that Harold reminded him of Howard at the age of twenty-one—red-haired, freckle-faced, boyishly handsome.

Over veal piccata Harold said he was eager to get back to the States to watch the NFL play-offs and Howard marveled, "You're so-o-oo butch!"

Harold blushed and asked whether they cared to come out to Cinecittà and visit Frankenheimer.

"I've known him forever," Gore said. "He used to direct my scripts at *Studio One*. The thing I'd like to ask John is what Bobby Kennedy told him that night he stayed at Frankenheimer's house just before he was assassinated."

"Afraid I can't help you there," Harold said.

When I arrived in 1991 with an assignment from *House & Garden* to do a piece about the grounds at La Rondinaia, Gore ribbed me, referring to the magazine as *Bitter Homes & Gardens*. But ever the autodidact, he had amassed information about the villa's original owner, Lord Grimthorpe, an amateur botanist who traveled the globe collecting specimens that would flourish in Ravello. Gore claimed that he carried on in Grimthorpe's tradition, although he acknowledged that Howard did the actual work.

Dutifully, Howard listed the flowers he had planted—gaillardia, dianthus, fuchsia, agapanthus, and tritoma.

"They sound like eye diseases." Gore restricted himself to strolling in the garden, where he said, "I think. Or I think I'm thinking. Then I sit beside the pool and read. I swim before lunch and come back at sundown to sit there again to watch the swallows sweep out of the evening sky and sip from the water."

It sounded idyllic, this scene I never had, and never would, witness. During my many visits to La Rondinaia, Gore never swam, never strolled the gardens, and never sat anyplace in the evening without a glass in hand. As for thinking he was thinking, that was a line straight out of *Myra Breckinridge*. For Gore, self-plagiarism was always the sincerest form of flattery.

After the interview, I suggested that we let *House & Garden* buy us dinner. Gore, who had by then begun writing his memoirs, was in a pensive, elegiac mood, and he chose Passetto, a once popular restaurant that had fallen out of favor. As we passed under the arch at the end of Passaggio Sinibaldi and crossed Corso del Rinascimento, Howard was gasping for breath, and Gore gimped along because of his bad knee. In Piazza Navona, wind blew mist off Bernini's Fountain of the Four Rivers, and waiters at Tre Scalini wore checkered tablecloths around their shoulders to ward off the cold.

At Passetto, the owner recognized Professore Vidal and treated the three of us with deference. But that didn't make up for the morose atmosphere. Most of the tables were empty, and among the sparse diners none appeared to be Italian.

"It's dead," Howard said, proclaiming the demise not just of the restaurant but of Rome itself. "The city's so bo-o—oring!"

Gore agreed that life here had become intolerable. The polluted air tormented his eyes and throat. The traffic on Largo Argentina ruined his sleep. And he could no longer abide the landlady who demanded an extortionate rent—$4,000 a month—for an apartment that had cost $270 a month when they'd moved in thirty years earlier. "The place would crumble if we didn't pour thousands into its upkeep."

Despite an apparent nonchalance about money, Gore was no pushover. Although he was generous with friends, he exercised petty economies in his day-to-day life. When the cook at La Rondinaia fixed fried chicken, he and Howard gnawed it down to the bones, then insisted she save them for the next day's *brodo*.

Gore clung to the old-school belief that one should never dip into capital—conservative wisdom he conceded he had violated in recent years. With the business model in publishing changing along with his confidence that he could continue to command million-dollar advances, he wondered whether there would be enough money to support Howard and him in the style to which they were accustomed. "The time to economize is now before the wolf is at the door."

"Rome's not worth it anymore," Howard said. "Not when we live in the apartment just a few months a year. We've had five burglaries, and every time it was up to me to fly in and deal with the police and the insurance people. It's a fucking nightmare."

They also decried the transformation of great swaths of the *centro storico* from residential areas into a dead zone of offices. To my astonishment, they talked of moving full-time to Ravello. It didn't seem possible, not after Gore had declared in *Fellini's Roma* that there was no better place to watch the end of the world than in a city that calls itself eternal. Did he believe Armageddon had been postponed? Or that it had already occurred?

After the meal, the headwaiter brought a bottle of Stolichnaya vodka encased in a clear plastic cube that resembled a block of ice. I assumed it was an *omaggio*, the sort of gift that favored customers often receive in Italy. Three thimble-size glasses accompanied the vodka; the headwaiter must have expected us to down a shot and depart. But Howard and Gore methodically drained the bottle to the last drop.

When the bill came, thirty dollars had been tacked on for after-dinner drinks. Gore was livid. I assured him it didn't matter.

It mattered to him, though, and as we retrieved our coats, he continued fuming. He noticed that the hatcheck girl was reading a bodice-ripping romance in English and lit into her. "You shouldn't be reading that drivel."

"What do you recommend?"

"You should be reading"—he flung an arm in my direction—"you should be reading him."

"Who's he?"

"His novel about Rome was made into a movie." Gore's voice died, and he did a double take. "Are you an American?"

"Yeah."

"Has it come to that?" he demanded, addressing the entire restaurant. "In my day Italians went to the States to work as hatcheck girls. Now Americans emigrate to Italy and don't even recognize their country's most famous novelist."

As he reeled out of Passetto, the poor girl asked, "Who are you?"

I should have told her, "Gore Vidal." Instead, I murmured, "Nobody you ever heard of," and hurried out with Howard.

We didn't catch up to Gore until he was on Via di Torre Argentina, stabbing his key at a door and swearing. "It's broken. It won't work."

"That's because we don't live there," Howard said.

Baffled, Gore glanced from the key to the lock and back again. Like a man trapped in a bad dream, he had lost track of where he was and where he belonged.

"We live in the next building," Howard said.

But not for long. They were about to depart Rome for good, for bad, and forever, thus ending a chapter in the city's long literary history.

Part II

NINE

Their move on St. Patrick's Day 1993 called to mind Hannibal, his elephants, and his Carthaginian army pouring down into Campania. Thousands of books, several suites of furniture, works of art, and cartons of clothing sped south in a truck, shepherded by half a dozen movers. Howard rode in a separate car, with fragile items and memorabilia, including photographs, some framed, others loose in boxes.

At La Rondinaia, Gore met him at the gate and hand carried one of his treasured possessions the rest of the way to the villa. He believed it to be a second-century Roman bust of Jove, beautiful despite its missing nose and chipped beard. The sight of a man bearing an ancient marble head along an allée of cypress and chestnut trees suggested some arcane ritual, an Attic ceremony of arrival.

Gore had bought the bust in New York City and imported it to Italy, thus reversing the usual route of classical antiquities, which were often smuggled out of the country and auctioned abroad. Now that it had returned to its country of origin, Gore didn't figure to be able to export it except through illegal subterfuge.

Gore also owned a first-century A.D. Roman mosaic of a hippocamp, a mythological creature with a horse's head and front hoofs and a coiled scaly fish's tail. It hung on the dining room wall at La Rondinaia, a dazzling accompaniment to many a bibulous meal. Always evasive about its provenance, Gore understood that he couldn't try to sneak it out of Italy without risking serious repercussions. The country was cracking down on dealers in antiquities and had started prosecuting private collectors and even foreign museums. But then, he and Howard declared that they never intended to leave Ravello.

In their exhilaration at taking up full-time (which wasn't to say legal) residence in the village, many problems must have seemed peripheral. Other problems were more pressing—not that Gore bothered about them, either. Although he regarded himself as an antiromantic, when it came to living arrangements, he made eccentric snap decisions that rivaled Arthur Rimbaud's settling in Abyssinia and selling guns to rebel tribes. Back in the 1940s, Gore had bought a ruined convent in Antigua, Guatemala, and holed up there for years before hepatitis nearly killed him. Now he and Howard were isolating themselves at La Rondinaia, imagining they had simplified their existence—"downsizing," as a retired couple in the States might have put it. But I feared that the move complicated their lives and jeopardized their safety.

Ravello, on the vertiginous heights of a serpentine road, boasted none of the amenities that senior citizens generally seek in their golden years. Hospitals and doctors were distant and unreliable. To complicate matters, Gore and Howard didn't own a car. I never once saw either of them drive. They depended on taxis to chauffeur them off the mountaintop. Gore used to be energetic enough to hike downhill to Amalfi, buy the daily newspapers, then catch a bus home. But those days were long gone. And Howard, whose recent X-rays had revealed lesions on his lungs, was in worse shape than Gore. Where he once paid village boys for sex, he now hired them to deal with daily chores that were beyond him.

A colorful town of revelers in summer, Ravello turned grim in winter. As I remembered from my stay, many of the hotels and restaurants shut down in November, and for the next five months a few lost souls rattled around on the windy streets. La Rondinaia, clinging to its cliff face, was accessible only by staircases that would have taxed a triathlete and a long path slippery with mud in wet weather. This was why the place had cost less than $300,000 when Gore bought it in the early 1970s. The previous owners had grown old and infirm and could no longer cope with a property that sprawled over seven terraced levels.

In an emergency, in those pre–cell phone, pre-Internet days, Gore and Howard had to hope that the landline was working or that one of them could hurry a quarter of a mile to the town square to sound the alarm. This nightmare scenario played out in 1996 when Gore returned from Los Angeles after an operation for the removal of five rectal polyps. Against his doctor's advice, he hopped a series of flights to Naples, drank heavily on the plane, and went on drinking at La Rondinaia to get to sleep. When he woke in the middle of the night, hemorrhaging badly, Howard was lucky to be able to track down an itinerant doctor who traveled between towns along the Amalfi coast. The doctor decided that Vidal needed to be hospitalized, and Howard rounded up four strong stretcher bearers to lug him to Ravello. By taxi they zigzagged for an hour along the coast to an emergency room in Salerno. Afterward, Gore wrote to a friend, "I nearly died . . . half of my red blood corpuscles went down the toilet."

Still, this close call didn't persuade them to reconsider living at La Rondinaia. Neither did the dangers posed by organized crime. The Camorra, a Neapolitan-based gang, had sunk its talons deep in the neighborhood, demanding protection money and a split of everything from the municipal budget to private real estate deals.

Gore and Howard weren't oblivious to the hold that thugs had on southern Italy. Even before their full-time move to La Rondinaia, the three of us were in Gore's studio watching CNN on May 23, 1992, when a bulletin interrupted the satellite broadcast to announce that on the airport road into Palermo a massive explosion had killed Giovanni Falcone, a special prosecutor who headed up an anti-Mafia investigation. The bomb cratered the four-lane *autostrada* and catapulted the armored car onto the roadside. Falcone's wife and bodyguards died with him.

To hammer home its contempt for the state and demonstrate its impunity, the Mafia let two months pass while a new special prosecutor, Paolo Borsellino, replaced Falcone. Then, in July, they assassinated him, too.

Yet Gore and Howard assumed they were safe. Living in a time of turmoil, in a place of foment, they behaved as they had after Pasolini's murder and all during the Red Brigades era—as though the problems of the rest of the world stopped at their property line. Even when the political landscape of Italy buckled in the 1990s and various parties, including the Christian Democrats, disintegrated during a national scandal called Tangentopoli—Bribe City— Gore remained complacently silent about corruption in his adopted country.

Three months after they relocated to Ravello, I interviewed Gore for *Architectural Digest*. *AD* had published a previous photo shoot of La Rondinaia when the Marrakech-based designer Bill Willis redecorated the interior. Now the magazine wanted an update, spiced with quotations about the celebrities Gore entertained at the villa. I was instructed to record the interview. This was standard Condé Nast procedure, but my editor stressed its greater urgency in the case of someone as litigious as Vidal.

The Stewarts drove me down from Rome, and we stopped at Caserta to buy a couple of kilos of *mozzarella di bufala* as a housewarming gift. The detour took longer than anticipated, and Gore was annoyed. "Oh, how you must have hurried," he said, each word wickedly serrated.

The Stewarts also brought him a fifth of twenty-five-year-old single malt scotch in a porcelain bottle nestled in a purple velvet-lined box. Gore accepted it grumpily and informed us he had made dinner reservations in Atrani at Zaccaria, a restaurant he and Howard regarded as their secret discovery. They contended that it had the best *spaghetti alle vongole veraci* in the world. It certainly had the largest portions; a waiter served us pasta and clams on a platter the size of a surfboard.

With it we downed five bottles of cold Lacryma Christi wine, and I knew there would be no interview that night. Gore was so unsteady on his pins, I wondered how much work would get done tomorrow, especially when we returned to La Rondinaia and kept drinking. Gore said that he'd save Donald and Luisa's premium scotch for "a special occasion, like my funeral."

"Jesus, not this again." Howard withdrew to his bedroom and minutes later rang on the intercom and told Gore to get to bed, too. He stayed put.

Donald and Luisa finished a nightcap, announced that they were exhausted, and left me alone with our host. I would have begged off, too, but I had a sudden premonition that this might be the night he drank himself to death. After he finished one bottle, he fumbled the porcelain decanter of single malt out of its velvet-lined box, hands shaking, fingers trembling. He barely managed to peel off the foil, then couldn't unscrew the cap. I didn't offer to help. I hoped he'd give up.

In frustration, he bashed the bottle against the fireplace, cracking off the cap, and drank straight from its jagged neck. All this time he continued talking. Or tried to. He sounded strangely maudlin—strange, that is, for a man who, even in his cups, usually avoided self-pity. He conceded that he was lonely and grateful I had kept him company. A forlorn figure in his chair, the bottle tucked between his thighs, he reminded me of Gustave von Aschenbach in Thomas Mann's *Death in Venice*. Tomorrow, I thought, he'll be dead, and word will go out around the world. There's no way he can survive this.

Perhaps I should have spent the night with him as a witness. But when Gore slipped into unconsciousness, I covered him as best I could with a throw rug. To steal a line from James Salter, he appeared to be "sleeping in the museum of his life," passed out in his study amid books and manuscripts, a welter of unanswered correspondence and pictures of himself with famous friends and enemies.

The next morning he woke hours before I did, and by noon, after what he swore had been a profitable session at his desk, he was ready to be interviewed. He mentioned nothing about the previous night, displayed no symptoms of a hangover, and peppily said, "See you at the pool. You look a little green around the gills. The water'll do you good."

I carried a cup of coffee and my tape recorder outside, where Donald was swimming laps and Luisa lay on a chaise longue tanning. In baggy shorts and a polo shirt, Gore had flopped under an umbrella. Sunlight slanting through canvas cast him in jaundiced light. His bare legs and feet looked bruised and sausage tight.

"Aren't you going to swim?" he asked me.

"Maybe later. What about you?"

"I like it right where I am."

"You look like a beached whale," Donald called from the water.

"Just waiting for the tide to carry my carcass out to sea."

Luisa suggested that he would benefit from exercise. He didn't have to swim, just walk from one end of the pool to the other. Aqua aerobics she called it. He replied that he didn't care to be aerobicized. But once the interview started, the old vigor and verbal acuity were rekindled. Not that he was, strictly speaking, responsive to my questions. For him the key to coping with journalists was to ignore what they asked and speak to whatever topic captured his fancy.

He told me, as he had before, that in 1948 he and Tennessee Williams explored the Amalfi coast in a secondhand army jeep. He repeated the joke about La Rondinaia inspiring him to take on a new book or film script to pay the bills. "In a sense," he said, "the completion of the swimming pool was the beginning of the process of leaving Rome."

He maintained that living in Ravello had brought his need for silence and solitude into balance with his social and professional obligations. The theme of harmony, of blending disparate elements, carried him along, easy as a leaf on a creek. He stressed that he had gathered under a single roof his most valued possessions—art, books, photographs. He spoke of the Aubusson tapestry that depicted a hunting party of Dutchmen slaying a wolf. It had hung in the *salone* in his penthouse. Now it adorned the *salone* here. "It's rather crude," he said, "but I've always liked it. And it brings together Rome and Ravello, uniting styles and houses."

Because a "shelter magazine" such as *Architectural Digest* dispensed practical advice along with its glossy pictures, I asked him to discuss what he and Howard had done to make the villa over into a year-round residence. The subject didn't engage him at more than a superficial level; he rattled off home improvements like a man reciting a laundry list. Double-glazed windows had been installed against winter winds, screens against summer mosquitoes. The gym, with its rusty weights, had been replaced by a library for the books he had shipped down from Rome. A porch next to his bedroom had been glassed in so that he could read there on cool days.

The villa, he said, had become "a full-service facility. Sometimes I don't leave it for days. With the satellite dish, I can follow events in the States, and there's a fax machine to send off reviews and essays."

He grew spirited as he described his collection of photographs. A snapshot of Charlton Heston in his *Ben-Hur* costume prompted a story about Paul Newman, who had originally been offered Heston's role. "Paul refused, because after *The Silver Chalice* he swore he would never act in a cocktail dress again."

He recounted how, as an honorary citizen of Ravello, he offici-
ated at local art shows and felt obliged to buy "a lot of wacky-
looking pictures. My favorite modern painter is Magritte, and a lot
of these people are painting Magritte pictures . . . very, very funny
ones that were done in all seriousness."

Following *AD*'s instructions, I asked about his famous guests.
To amuse Donald and Luisa, and maybe keep himself interested,
Gore recalled a few louche anecdotes, knowing I didn't dare include them in my article and that *Architectural Digest* wouldn't print
them if I did. He skewered one grand name after another and was
particularly venomous about Alberto Moravia. "Since he never lifted
a finger for me," he said, "I made it a point to do nothing for him."

"Attaboy, Gore," Donald called out.

He said that Rudolf Nureyev, who had died of AIDS six
months earlier, had often visited La Rondinaia and always stripped
off his clothes and leaped naked into the pool, plunging deep, re-
surfacing, and spouting water like a porpoise. "By then the disease
had withered his whole body, except for his legs and that enormous
cock of his."

Nureyev had owned a tiny island off the Amalfi coast, Gallo
Lungo, formerly the home of another Russian dancer, Léonide
Massine, and before him the famous impresario Sergei Diaghilev.
A doctor flew in regularly from Paris to give Nureyev blood trans-
fusions, which energized him in short spurts. He repaired then to
his studio in a tower. It was a heartbreaking scene Gore described—a
dying man dancing, practicing the repertoire of leaps that used to
send him soaring for audiences the world over but that now barely
lifted him off the ground.

On their last afternoon together, Gore told how he had walked
Nureyev to the gate at La Rondinaia. They both realized they
would never see each other again. Nureyev made the sign of the
cross, and by Gore's account he inscribed a Russian cross, a kind of
X mark, on his dying friend's chest. As he forcefully demonstrated

this on my chest, I thought it possible that Nureyev had felt rubbed out rather than blessed.

I admitted I had trouble envisioning Vidal, the vehement atheist, playing a high priest's role. He drawled, "Whatever the situation requires."

It was a good story, which is no doubt why he included it almost verbatim in his second volume of memoirs, *Point to Point Navigation*. He omitted, however, any mention of Nureyev's cock, and he deleted another detail he revealed that day. "They say you can't catch AIDS easily. They say chlorine'll kill it off. But just to be on the safe side, Howard and I drained the pool after Rudi left, then had it refilled."

That evening we ate at La Rondinaia under a cut-glass chandelier, in a dazzle of splintered light, seated in the brass embossed chairs festooned with rams' heads, which Gore again swore had been props from *Ben-Hur*. Afterward, we watched a videocassette of Bette Davis starring in *The Catered Affair*, a 1950s movie that Gore had adapted from a Paddy Chayefsky TV script. And while we watched, he recalled Bette Davis strolling down a hotel corridor in Hollywood and bumping into Ava Gardner, who exclaimed, "Oh my God, you're my favorite woman in the world." To which Davis replied, "Of course, I am, dear," and kept on going.

The black-and-white film, the laughing company of Donald and Luisa, Howard and Gore, reminded me of childhood evenings when my family, like millions of Americans, had gathered in front of a television for a few hours of innocent fun. But as the movie ended and Gore switched from white wine to scotch, things took a discomfiting tangent. I had then known him for eighteen years. The Stewarts had been his friends for three decades. Howard had lived with him for forty-three years. So it was with shock that we listened to him tell a tale we had never heard before, one about "the love of his life," a teenage classmate at St. Albans. The boy's name was Jimmie Trimble, and like so many of his generation he had joined the military right after high school, undergone cursory training, and shipped out to the Pacific, where he died on Iwo Jima.

This was utterly unlike Gore's other reminiscences. Even when he was drunk—especially when he was drunk!—there was usually a scorpion sting attached to his tales. But he spoke about Jimmie Trimble with an absolute absence of irony.

"Love of my life"—that wasn't a Gore Vidal line. He had long claimed he didn't believe in love; there was no such thing. He swore he had never loved anybody and routinely refused to indulge in sentiment, much less sentimentality. Yet here he was professing that Jimmie and he "were like two halves that formed a whole. We fit together perfectly." He portrayed them as Achilles and Patro-clus. Or like Tom Sawyer and Huck Finn, whiling away summer days at Merrywood, playing in the woods, swimming in the Po-tomac, untroubled about treacherous currents or snakes.

He insisted that what made them unlike the average angst-ridden, messy adolescents was their complete lack of guilt about "belly rubbing." Their mutual pleasure—the mention of mutual pleasure was another first coming from Gore—felt so natural, so carefree, they never needed to discuss or analyze what they did. When he went on to describe roller-skating with Jimmie on the driveway at Merrywood "holding each other's cock," I thought per-haps he was building toward a punch line. It was all a setup, a scene from Norman Rockwell as rendered by Lenny Bruce—this image of two barely pubescent boys playing crack the whip on wheels. But Gore remained deadly earnest.

Where Jimmie had been a star athlete, the best pitcher in the history of St. Albans's baseball team, Gore had been bookish, al-though by no means a top student. Totally absorbed in reading and writing and debating his future—should he become president or a bestselling author?—he had floated indifferently through his classes. Still, Jimmie respected him as an equal, he said, just as Gore respected his fastball-throwing friend.

Sturdily built and about the same height, the two of them had stood naked and pressed together until they both enjoyed thunderous orgasms. "His sweat," Gore said, "smelled like honey."

"What does honey smell like?" Donald asked.

"It smells like Jimmie Trimble."

"Gore, you're drunk," Howard said. "Go to bed." Howard disappeared into his room, tarried half an hour, then as usual buzzed the intercom. Gore refused to answer it.

Like Howard, I wondered how much of this monologue was a sort of soppy delirium tremens. A variation on his late-night reveries a decade earlier about having a daughter by a woman he refused to name. It struck me as an alternative plot speculation, not necessarily an authentic revelation.

On the other hand, Gore was writing his memoirs. Had that shaken loose memories of Jimmie Trimble? Something might have happened, and maybe it was as sexually charged and life altering as Gore would have us believe. Still, the idea that his personal history hinged on a fleeting teenage love smacked to me of romance fiction.

The tale about Jimmie Trimble raised questions that could never be answered. Most of them would never be asked, much less subjected to fact-checking. Passing straight from Gore's mouth onto the pages of *Vanity Fair*, then into his memoirs, and then with scant revision into his authorized biography, his account of the experience sounded like the sort of schmaltz he had mocked in Tennessee Williams, whom he accused of being a charter member of the "school of Elizabeth Barrett Browning; I shall but love thee better after death."

After Donald and Luisa went to bed and I was alone with Gore, he became combative and petulant, accusing me of not believing him about Jimmie Trimble.

"What does it matter what I believe?" I asked.

"I don't want you thinking I'm like Truman Capote—a world-class liar."

I muttered something to the effect that we all need stories that explain our lives. This didn't satisfy Gore; again he bristled that I was accusing him of lying.

"Not at all," I said. "But the way you tell it . . ." I trailed off, realizing it was as insulting to belittle his style as to doubt his truthfulness.

I started over. "What if Philip Roth told you his whole life turned on his love for a high school cheerleader? How would you react?"

He responded with the sort of side step a politician might deploy. "Philip Roth's a shit. As a favor for my good friend Claire Bloom, I got him into the New York Athletic Club when he had a bad back and needed a place to swim. Do you think he's ever thanked me? Not a word."

The next day, on the drive back to Rome, Donald and Luisa Stewart acknowledged their own doubts about Jimmie Trimble. They wondered why Gore, who never displayed any hesitation to divulge intimacies about his mother's infantile vagina and his father's three testicles, would have held his silence on this subject for half a century.

TEN

In 1995, after six years in the States, Linda and I moved to London, and a few weeks after we landed, Gore Vidal passed through town on a publicity tour for *Palimpsest*. To surprise him, I popped into Hatchard's bookstore on Piccadilly and stood in line with a crowd of fans waiting for the author to autograph his memoir.

Howard, who sat off to the side of the signing table, spotted me and gave a tired wave of the hand. He looked drawn and pale, his freckles dull copper specks on a paper-white face.

Gore, who had turned seventy in early October, didn't look much better. His shirt buttons were stretched to the popping point, and his blazer hung open, exposing a swagged belly. His shoulders were dusted with dandruff, and his parchment-dry skin had a permanent crease on the right cheek.

I figured the promotional tour must have been long and arduous and that whatever spare time they had in London they would spend with British friends—Princess Margaret, Lord This, Lady That. I planned to pay my respects and be on my way. But Gore invited Linda and me to dinner that night at the Connaught hotel.

On the tube ride back to our apartment in Hampstead, I riffled through the memoir and admired the photographs of Gore's family and famous acquaintances. Then, following his example—before reading biographies and autobiographies, he confessed, he always looked for his own name—I flipped to the index. Because *Palimpsest* focused on the first thirty-nine years of his life, I didn't actually expect to be part of the story. But I was bewildered to notice no mention of Mickey Knox, who had been instrumental in Gore's reconciliation with Norman Mailer. Surely Mickey deserved a sentence or two.

Ditto Donald and Luisa Stewart. Although longtime friends, and in Donald's case the contact at *Playboy* who had brokered assignments for Gore, they were curiously absent. So were Steve and Joan Geller, Bob and Beverly Katz, and the rest of the old Roman crowd. Not even George Armstrong, Gore's traveling companion, typist, and cruising partner, made a token appearance.

Because Gore believed that "palimpsest" was "a word nobody will know," he took pains in a preface to spell out its meaning: "'Paper, parchment, etc., prepared for writing on and wiping out again, like a slate' . . . 'a parchment, etc., which has been written upon twice; the original writing having been rubbed out.'" He concluded, "This is pretty much what my kind of writer does anyway. Starts with life; makes a text; then a *re*-vision—literally, a second seeing."

His stated motive for writing *Palimpsest* was to set the record straight. Fed up with reading about himself in other people's books and "finding a stranger masquerading with my name," he had also grown impatient with Walter Clemons, his authorized biographer. In five years, the ex-*Newsweek* staffer had failed to produce a word. Under pressure from his publisher, Little, Brown, Clemons repeatedly promised to submit chapters of his manuscript, then missed every self-imposed deadline.

Finally, Clemons swore he would deliver three hundred pages by February 1993, and when he failed to do so, Gore switched to a different biographer, Fred Kaplan, who took for granted that he would get access to Clemons's files. But Clemons died in 1994 of a diabetic seizure, and his interview transcripts and notes ended up sealed by his executor.

The great irony was that Gore, by choosing Walter Clemons, who he believed would be compliant, had got stuck with an incompetent. Eager to avoid being Blotnered—that is, driven to an early grave—he picked a biographer who died prematurely himself and dragged the project down with him. Small wonder then that Gore decided to write his own memoir while the new authorized biographer started research from scratch.

Howard and Gore were drunk when Linda and I joined them in their suite at the Connaught. Room service had sent up a magnum of Veuve Clicquot and a pot of caviar, much of which dribbled down Gore's shirtfront, along with hard-boiled egg yolk and toast crumbs. He razzed me that my hair was thinning and my waistline was thickening.

"Look who's fucking talking," Howard hooted.

At dinner, Gore ordered for everybody—quail eggs, roast beef and Yorkshire pudding, a new wine with each course, and spotted dick, a dessert he favored for the name alone. He didn't eat a bite of it, content to consume his sugar in liquid form.

The next day Gore undoubtedly woke early and went straight to work. I rose late with a quaking belly and set about reading *Palimpsest*. John Cheever claimed that good writing can cure anything, including the common cold. It was certainly tonic for my hangover. The memoir was a miracle every bit as mysterious as Gore's ironclad constitution. A miracle and a mystery and a magnificent display of mandarin prose.

Although he had been handicapped by depression and drinking, hamstrung by lawsuits, distracted by bickering with editors, and beset by ill health and the infirmities of aging, *Palimpsest* was a bravura performance, in many respects his best book in decades. Line after line, the sentences had the snap of a dominatrix's whip. Alternately cruelly funny and funnily cruel, his takedown of Harold Acton was a model of misdirection. He synopsized Acton's *More*

Memoirs of an Aesthete as "the ongoing story of a long and marvelously uninteresting life . . . a work to be cherished for its remarkable number of unaesthetic misprints and misspellings."

Nowhere, though, was his wit better displayed than in caustic recollections of his mother, Nina Gore Vidal Auchincloss Olds. "She *hated* selfishness in others, and saw it everywhere, especially in me. Ominously, I would be warned 'to turn over a new leaf'— this usually preceded my being sent off to yet another school, even farther from 'home' than the last. 'From here on out,' Nina would announce, at regular intervals for the rest of her life, 'I'm looking out for number one.'"

On the level of pure—or impure—gossip, *Palimpsest* achieved what should have been impossible. Despite Gore's protestations that "I have never had much interest in the sexual lives of real people," he sank his arms up to his elbows in an ooze of prurience yet never sounded hypocritical, perhaps because his candor was at such odds with other people's pharisaical posturing. And it never sounded sleazy because of the Parnassian diction with which, for instance, he rendered the scene of Jackie Kennedy in Paris losing her virginity in an elevator stalled between floors.

Gore was blunt about his own sexual escapades. Asked by Allen Ginsberg what he had done with Jack Kerouac, he said, "I fucked him."

"I don't think that he would have liked that," Ginsberg replied.

"Maybe that was the point."

Refusing to court approval, empathy, or pity, Gore was determined—or so he wanted it to appear—to reveal precisely what he was like and to prove that other people were no different and no better, regardless of what they pretended or how thoroughly they fooled themselves.

As I read on and on—the book was more than four hundred densely printed pages—the mordant Vidal voice seldom varied, the all-knowing tone rarely modulated. His persona as the guru of cynicism, the yoga master of world-weariness, was effective in short spurts but grew monotonous at book length, and I was puzzled why so many of the emotions I had witnessed in him over the years had been deleted from this draft of his life. Where was the anger, the rankling resentment at his exclusion, the humiliation, the professional and personal disappointments, the drinking, and the yearning for death?

Instead, there were passages about pleasures I had never known him to enjoy. "Today, I wonder why I am so content, inhabiting as I do a body so keen to disassemble. Then I realize why, perfect day to one side: I do not want anything. I am past all serious desire for anything—at the moment, anyway. The Buddha was right: To want is to suffer."

This Zen koan set awkwardly with the man who just the night before at the Connaught had drunk himself to the brink of unconsciousness. However successful as literature and riveting as gossip, *Palimpsest*, it occurred to me, wasn't so much a memoir as a novel with a thoroughly unreliable narrator. It was performance art, another Gore Vidal extravaganza calculated to mislead readers and perhaps himself. Endlessly shuffling and reshuffling familiar anecdotes from his essays, he showed no awareness that as he shunted the stock footage of his life from one medium to another, there might need to be a reassessment, that material churned out to meet a journalistic deadline might benefit by a reappraisal, or that the passage of time or the death of a literary or political figure might call for a reevaluation.

In conversation, Gore referred to *Palimpsest* as his "me-more," explaining, "It's more about me." But it contained little that he hadn't written about before. Nor was it in any respect a palimpsest. Rather than a re-vision of a previous draft, it was a mash-up of snippets from his published work. Chapters about Tennessee Williams, Truman Capote, the Kennedys, Gore's father and grandfather, William F. Buckley, and Johnny Carson had been scissored and pasted from his clippings. Even a charming anecdote about his Roman apartment and the surrounding neighborhood had been appropriated word for word from an article for *Architectural Digest*.

The most deeply felt material dealt with Jimmie Trimble, and while it expanded on what Gore told Howard, Donald, Luisa, and me that night in Ravello, his strenuous effort to infuse an adolescent sexual dalliance with universal significance had the unfortunate effect of increasing my doubts. It struck me as, if not a fantasy, then a rationalization for his lifelong failure to express love.

When he described Jimmie as a "Rosebud" figure, I remembered the piece he had written about William Randolph Hearst, the model for *Citizen Kane*. In it, Gore claimed that Hearst referred to Marion Davies's clitoris as Rosebud. Moreover, in *Myron*, the sequel to *Myra Breckinridge*, Gore used "American rosebuds" as a synonym for penises. Was he signaling that Jimmie Trimble was an inside joke, a sexual allusion—or should that be "illusion"?—a postmodern send-up? Or had he forgotten his earlier references to "Rosebud"? Alcohol does scramble the brain. What other explanation was there for Gore's insistence in a later interview that he had served "in the American army, in the Pacific at the time they bombed Hiroshima and then Nagasaki," when the memoir indicated that he was by then safely back in the States recovering from a case of frostbite he contracted in Alaska?

In a convoluted text distinguished by cinematic cuts and time bends, an author might be forgiven for losing track of a few details. But quite apart from quibbles over minor errors, the greatest flaw in *Palimpsest* was Gore's refusal to come to grips with his inner life, with the painful traumas he suffered in private while he sustained the impression in public of perfect equanimity.

A last point about *Palimpsest*: Its publication persuaded Gore to violate a self-declared embargo on print interviews and allow Andrew Solomon from *The New York Times Magazine* to visit him in Ravello. By now the *Times* had adapted to the zeitgeist and quit regarding gays as pariahs. Solomon went so far as to admire the shapeliness of Gore's ankles and to remark that "his manner of well-bred control is most engaging and you can see at once why so many thousands of people slept with him (cf. *Palimpsest*) and why so many others wanted to (op. cit.)." This line must have set Orville Prescott, the late book reviewer for the daily *Times*, spinning in his grave.

Solomon quoted—and, just as amazing, the *Times* printed—Gore's candid declaration of his erotic inclinations. "If you're not in the business of baby making, the anonymous or paid encounter is far more satisfactory . . . If it's somebody that you know, there's nothing exciting about it at all to me; if I know somebody in one capacity, I certainly have no interest in the other."

Solomon wasn't so besotted, however, that he couldn't be objective about Gore's work. Of his historical fiction about the classical past, he remarked that it can be "tedious" and not as strong as the American narratives from *Burr* through *Empire* and *Hollywood*. Of his trademark flights of fancy, such as *Myra Breckinridge* and *Live from Golgotha*, he wrote, "They are evil satires that outpoststructuralize the deconstructionists; when they are not maudlin, confusing and overwritten, they are gloriously uninhibited and very funny."

Gore's gift as a comedian often got lost in interviews, but Solomon was on his wavelength and had the wisdom to step aside and let him riff. About his mother Gore quipped, "She confessed that rage made her orgasmic. I forgot to ask her if sex ever did."

Mocking America's obsession with national security, he told Solomon, "Now we have an enemy-of-the-month club. If it's not Noriega, it's Bishop in Grenada; Qaddafi, whose eyeliner is very ominous; Saddam, just like Hitler. When they get into their bunkers they always find a copy of *Mein Kampf*, a portrait of Hitler, women's underdrawers—which they wear—a couple of dead Boy Scouts and three mistresses."

Solomon observed that while Vidal could be stern, "he is not (as his reputation would have it) cold; he has sometimes aspired to but has never fully achieved the statesman's indifference. He is a circumspect romantic . . . The pathos and elegance of his work lie in the conflict between the bearing of a visionary if unelectable politician and the sensibility of a fine writer—between an accomplished distance and palpably emotional self-recognition."

To my disappointment, Solomon, a survivor of a crippling depression that he would chronicle in his award-winning memoir, *The Noonday Demon*, didn't notice, or didn't care to divulge, Vidal's dysthymia. Still, his profile for *The New York Times Magazine* gave me deep delight, almost as if I had written it myself. I only hoped it hadn't come too late to give Gore some satisfaction.

ELEVEN

In April 1998, I had an assignment from an embryonic magazine, *Notorious*, named not after the 1946 film starring Cary Grant and Ingrid Bergman but in honor of the rap singer Biggie Smalls, a.k.a. Notorious B.I.G., who had been gunned down the previous year during a drive-by shooting in L.A. His pal Sean "Puff Daddy" Combs financed the enterprise and commissioned an interview with Gore Vidal for its inaugural issue.

Somehow *Notorious* contrived to die as dead as Biggie Smalls before its first issue hit the newsstand. But the trip to Ravello was memorable. Our younger son, Marc, came along with Linda and me. Then a senior at the American School in London, he had read *1876* and was eager to meet the author. I warned Marc that Gore might confuse him with his older brother, Sean, and call him "the Dwarf." I decided against mentioning that Gore remembered Marc as a child in Rome wearing a kimono. Ever since then he presumed the boy had grown up to be a cross-dresser.

Gore laid down the usual caveat that I write nothing about his having a receding hairline. And there was a new demand—that I fax my questions in advance. He would respond in writing, after which the Q&A had to run unedited.

As we drove south, rain dogged us everyplace except in the

mountains, where wet snow fell on forsythia blossoms. By the time we reached Ravello, a gale had wrung the dampness out of the sky, but the air was raw and wintry. Abiding strictly by the calendar, Italians had switched off the heat back in March, and our room at the Hotel Palumbo was as cold as a meat locker.

Bundling up in overcoats, Linda and I hiked to La Rondinaia while Marc remained at the hotel. Wind rattled through the chestnut and cypress trees, shaking water from low-hanging limbs. Dead leaves and flower petals circulated in the swimming pool. From a distance the villa looked deserted, desolate. In Gore's study, where embers glowed feebly in the fireplace, a fierce chill stole from the bare floors and walls into our bones. The windows were wide open in the vain hope of a warming breeze; the temperature inside was the same as outside.

As always the writing table spilled over with pens and pencils and yellow legal pads, manuscript pages, letters, and two portable Olivetti typewriters. A pale cat with hairless pink ears lay curled amid the chaos. Gore said the cat had caught cancer from his halogen lamp.

He and Howard sprawled at either end of a sofa, highball glasses in hand. Normally, they drank wine with lunch but never hard liquor before sundown. They were both quite drunk and urged us to join them. "It'll warm your blood," Howard said. "Nothing else in this fucking house will."

"What news of Martin Amis?" Gore asked. Aware that I played tennis with Amis in London, he presumed, as did other people, that I knew England's preeminent novelist far better than I did. Whenever interviewers inquired, I limited myself to comments about Amis's impeccable line calls and relentless retrieving. Gore used to refer to him as "Little Martin," but after Amis reviewed *Palimpsest* enthusiastically, he dropped the diminutive.

"Martin's brilliant," I replied, putting on my best British accent.

"What news of America?" A far better mimic than I, Gore affected a cornpone accent. "There's a rumor Slick Willy Clinton's not going to beat this Monica Lewinsky scandal. They say his baby gravy's all over that gal's dress."

"You mean his boy butter." Howard tossed a chunk of olive wood into the fireplace. It fell like a brick, setting off an eruption of sparks, but no warmth at all. Howard sagged back onto the sofa. "Fucking house," he said. "Fucking cold."

"Maybe it would help to shut the windows," Linda suggested.

"Then the smoke'll smother us."

"This may be our last winter here," Gore said. "We're thinking about moving into town."

"Rome?"

"No, Ravello. During the worst months, we'll check into a hotel."

Howard giggled at the notion of relocating a quarter of a mile to a village that in winter was as dead as church Latin. "You'd never guess we had a perfectly nice, perfectly well-heated house in the Hollywood Hills."

"All my stuff is here," Gore protested. "My books, the art."

"So ship it back to the States," Howard said.

Gore glanced at the clock. I guessed they were expecting guests and wanted Linda and me out of the way. But when I mentioned going back to the Palumbo, they begged us to stick around.

"When did Barbara promise to call?" Howard asked.

"Midday, New York time," Gore said. "As soon as she gets word." Given the gravity of his voice, he might have been waiting for a medical diagnosis. But it emerged that he had been short-listed for a literary prize. He wouldn't say which one, and he downplayed his chances of winning. Still he stayed in the freezing study, and we stayed with him, waiting for Barbara Epstein to ring with what he guaranteed would be bad news.

It was dark and Howard had switched on the lights by the time the call came. Gore languidly answered the phone, languidly listened, languidly thanked her, then languidly placed the receiver on its cradle. He peered into the fireplace at one or two live coals in a heap of ashes. He waggled his forefinger in the Italian fashion, miming no.

"Fucking people, they don't deserve you," Howard said.

Gore stood up, straightened his blazer, and stepped over to the writing table, each gesture a concerted effort to demonstrate that he couldn't care less about the lost prize. He picked up a copy of *The Nation* and passed it to Linda. "Here's an article of mine that might interest you. Why don't you read it?"

"Sure. Marc's at the hotel. He'll want to read it, too. He's a great fan of yours."

"I'd rather you read it now. Out loud if you don't mind."

"The whole thing?" Linda asked.

"Yes." Then coldly polite, "If you don't mind." With that he settled in for the next half hour and listened to his own prose, rigid in his refusal to admit he was upset.

Afterward, he thanked Linda and said he and Howard would join us for dinner at the Sasso, a new luxury hotel. I insisted that *Notorious* pick up the bill. Then, before leaving, I asked whether he had answered the questions I faxed him. Gore assured me he would attend to them tonight and have the interview in my hands by morning. Considering his current mood, this struck me as improbable.

The Hotel Sasso (subsequently renamed Palazzo Avino) was accessible from Ravello's main square via a long oleander-lined staircase, the Viale Richard Wagner. Set between the Palumbo and the Caruso hotels, the Sasso was an upscale, updated establishment sleekly inserted into a twelfth-century villa. With its uncluttered decor and immense windows, it had Ravello's standard—that is to say, astounding—views of the sea. But its greatest luxury that raw spring night was its efficient heating system.

Linda, Marc, and I arrived early, only to discover Gore already in the bar sipping a martini. He explained that Howard didn't feel well and had remained at home.

The hotel manager, aware of hosting the town's most celebrated citizen, ushered us into the restaurant, Rossellinis. "None of the local tomato sauce and mozzarella goop," Gore said. "This place is shooting for the stars—Michelin stars." And indeed it would go on to win two of them.

With the manager hovering, the maître d' proposed that we let him serve a selection of *assaggini*—sample tastings of the restaurant's specialties. And *con permesso* he would choose the wine, a new bottle with each mini-course.

Gore signaled for him to bring it on—the *assaggini* and the wine and another martini as an *aperitivo* for him. Between one thing and another, between one bottle and the next, I have no clear recollection of the meal, except that there was too much of it and that I feared the feast would cost far more than my fee from *Notorious*.

Money, however, wasn't all I had on my mind. I tried to keep track of how much wine Gore poured for Marc, who, at the age of seventeen, was hard put to digest the alcohol on top of Gore's diatribe against RAI TV. Apparently, a producer had promised to shoot a profile of him and, after squandering days of his time, had delivered nothing except excuses.

By midnight, five empty bottles were strewn like dead soldiers on a tablecloth stained with bloodred wine. When the manager suggested an after-dinner drink, Gore requested grappa and announced that he and Howard were considering Hotel Sasso as their winter residence.

The manager said, "Please accept tonight's meal as an *omaggio*, a small token of the warm welcome that awaits you and your friend."

By now the restaurant was empty; waiters were stacking chairs.

When I offered to walk him back to La Rondinaia, Gore protested—although it was unclear exactly what he protested. Was it the end of the evening? Would he rather make it to the villa alone? Or was he desperate not to return to those icy rooms and the scene of this afternoon's setback?

He was as close to complete incoherence and physical collapse as I had ever seen him. With Marc's help, I hauled him to his feet and guided him out of the Sasso and into the cold air. That revived him a bit. "Lemme go," he slurred.

He lurched down Viale Richard Wagner, thudded to his knees, and bounced up like a jack-in-the-box. Determined to make it on his own steam, he reeled from oleander to oleander, lamppost to lamppost, grabbing one, groping for the next. On level ground in the square, having nothing else to hang on to, he sagged against me, all 230 pounds of him. It felt as if I were pulling a plow over the cobblestones past the bar Al San Domingo and down the dark, bumpy path to one gate, then another. He fumbled the keys from his blazer pocket, but I had to do the unlocking, which meant letting Gore flop onto his butt.

When we reached La Rondinaia, he kissed me smack on the mouth, for the first and only time in thirty-seven years, and as he disappeared into the villa, it dawned on me as it had on previous occasions, tonight's the night he'll die.

Again I was wrong. More than just wrong, ridiculously off base. In the morning he delivered a clean typescript of the Q&A. Because *Notorious*, instead of Gore Vidal, died, *The Independent* published the answers that displayed his astonishing recuperative powers as well as his wit and insight into sex and politics.

MM: During Watergate, you said you couldn't wait to get out of bed each morning to get your daily fill of the scandal's latest developments. Do you feel the same about Clinton and Zippergate?

GV: There is a certain dull monotony to the attacks on Clinton. For one thing, he himself is well liked, and no one save the mad (all right—half the American people should probably serve some time in a cloistered bin) finds him at all like Nixon, who at every full moon became a werewolf, to the applause, no doubt, of the binnable half.

Kenneth Starr, of course, is seriously unhinged in the Elmer Gantry snake-oil-selling Jesus-quoting southern way, and I suppose when he finally cracks up on television and bites deep into Tom Brokaw's pretty jugular, my jaded attention will finally be caught.

MM: You don't seem to view Clinton's alleged peccadilloes with the same seriousness as Nixon's.

GV: Watergate was the subversion of the Constitution by an incumbent president. Clinton's sole crime was a disinclination to confess to a grand jury that he likes the odd blow job, a taste he shares with most of the male population. In respectable societies, gentlemen—and ladies—never discuss their sex lives in public, and if confronted with the subject, they are expected—nay, suborned—to lie. In a survey in a recent book, *The Day America Told the Truth*, over 90 percent of U.S. citizens confessed to being habitual liars.

Bad lawyers have made a fetish out of perjury, something no other country bothers much with unless some real crime—like murder—is being investigated. Clinton should have refused to respond to Starr's literally impertinent questions about his private life.

If Congress or Supreme Court were then to order him to respond, he should, under executive power and through the Justice Department, put the whole lot under oath to discuss their sex lives. The traditions and filing systems of J. Edgar Hoover still live at the FBI and Langley! This should have a restraining effect.

Finally, I would seriously entertain a charge of treason against Starr for trying to overthrow We the People, the source of all legitimacy, by preventing Clinton from the execution of that office we elected him to.

MM: To what extent is the sex life of the president a legitimate political concern?

GV: If he was a sex criminal—rapist, blackmailer—of course it would be relevant. But what consenting adults do, etc., etc.

MM: In your memoir *Palimpsest* you pointed out that the variety and intensity of John Kennedy's sex life bore some resemblance to your own. You both seem to have subscribed to the theory that one should never turn down an opportunity to be on TV or to have sex. Do you believe that part of Clinton's alleged promiscuity is simply a matter of a famous man having more opportunities?

GV: Obviously. Also, the drive that gets one to the peculiar state of "famous" in a very peculiar country like the United States—superstitious, bigoted, and, worst of all, garrulous—is apt to be accompanied by a strong sex drive. The press acts as if Clinton uses his high office to get girls. It is the other way round—it is the high profile that is like catnip to women. Watch them crowd about Leonardo Di-Caprio. Those pubescent girls are going to eat him raw one day—*The Bacchae* was a realistic play.

MM: If famous men do have more opportunities, was Marx—Karl, not Groucho—correct to say a change in quantity is a change in quality?

GV: That's one way of looking at it—though most of us prefer quantity to start with. Boys are meant to squirt as often as possible with as many different partners as possible. Girls are designed to take nine months to lay an egg. Different wavelengths. Groucho Marx at the end of his life was asked if he had it to do all over again, what would he do differently? "Try another position."

MM: According to news reports, which may amount to no more than slightly refined gossip, President Clinton's encounters with Monica Lewinsky consisted of oral sex. The invariable assumption is that he was the receiver. Is it possible that as the national leader he was more concerned about the young woman's pleasure and was the giver?

GV: Richard Morris must rule on who is giving the pleasure and who is the taker. I suspect that Clinton doesn't much care for Warm Mature Relationships with Warm Caring Women. Hence, an addiction to the impersonal blow job.

MM: In his recent book about John F. Kennedy, Seymour Hersh suggests that the president's complicated sex life left him open to blackmail, brought him into contact with low-life hookers and mobsters, and definitely affected his conduct in office. Do you agree?

GV: Yes. Though the Giancana connection was forged long before they shared Ms. Exner.

MM: To what extent might Clinton be accused of similar offenses?

GV: Clinton, as far as we know, is not into crime. The Kennedys, thanks first to Honey Fitz, mayor of Boston, and then to his son-in-law Joe Kennedy, were deeply involved with the Mafia. That was the heart of the Hersh book, but Marilyn Monroe got the headlines as the media cannot bear anything actually true because, sooner or later, they are going to be fingered, too.

MM: You've often questioned the cult that surrounds the Kennedys. Why do you think the public continues to care? And does the public's obsession with the Kennedys explain your ongoing willingness to write about the family?

GV: I wrote about them briefly in *Palimpsest*. After all, Jackie and I were brought up in the same house by the same people. In thirty-eight years I've written exactly three pieces about the Kennedys. Hardly obsessive.

MM: In your autobiography, you claim that your relationship with Howard Austen has endured for decades because it's nonsexual. Could you address this? Do you view sex as antithetical to an ongoing relationship? Or the reverse?

GV: I've made it a rule never to have sex with friends. One can always find sex, as Bill will tell you, but one doesn't find friends that easily, as Bill will also tell you.

MM: You've expressed dissatisfaction with journalists and their tendency to turn interviews into diatribes against you. Is it possible President Clinton is partly a victim of the same sort of misrepresentation?

GV: When Hillary Clinton came to call on me a few summers ago, we did nothing but trade stories on what people had invented about us. It is not the "diatribes" one minds. It is the quotation of something you never said. This need not be the result of malice. Incompetence is also a journalistic failing.

MM: What do you see as Clinton's lasting legacy? If nothing else, has he changed the nature of political discourse?

GV: The post-Truman presidents are all fading away, as our American empire is doing—though too slowly for my taste. Since we have elections but no politics, Clinton has been the opening wedge for a truly great diversion, the candidates' sex life. This really keeps us away from discussing politics, a subject the owners of the country fear.

What is real politics? Who collects what money from whom to spend on whom for what. That's all there is to it, but no politician in the United States dares address that subject for fear we'll discover who bought him and for how much—not to mention how the military got us five trillion dollars into debt.

TWELVE

In February 1999 our paths crossed in Paris, where Linda and I met Gore and Howard for a meal of "hooters"—their intentional mispronunciation of *huîtres*, the French word for oysters. The evening began with drinks in their suite at the hotel Le Bristol, and for a while—a long while—it looked as if we would never make it out to dinner.

Finally, Linda protested that she was starving and steered us across the street to a brasserie where we ordered "hooters" and *steak frites* and a couple bottles of Beaujolais. After consuming a dozen oysters each, Howard and Gore did little more than push food around their plates. Gore worked steadily at the wine, then switched to scotch. "We're selling La Rondinaia," he announced with no prelude.

"You mean we're trying to sell it," Howard corrected him.

I wasn't entirely surprised. I had wondered how long they could hold out in the isolation and inconvenience of Ravello. Still, it worried me that Gore would be cutting his ties to a place where he had worked well. The move threatened not just his writing but his morale.

When I said as much, he replied that they weren't leaving anytime soon. It could take years to find a buyer for such an expensive property in an area as idiosyncratic as southern Italy.

"Meanwhile, this isn't for publication," he said.

"How're you going to keep it quiet?" Howard asked. "When people hear your price, it'll be all over the papers."

"What are you asking?"

"Fourteen million euros," Gore said.

That was $17 million at the then-current exchange rate—a tidy capital gain of $16.7 million. The potential tax liability, involving fiscal systems as inscrutable as Italy's and as stringent as the States', would require complex and discreet negotiations. And there were other looming problems. Gore feared certain interests—"criminal elements," Howard spelled it out—might try to muscle in. There was also a chance that the Belle Arti commission would declare La Rondinaia part of the national patrimony and demand to purchase it at a price it deemed to be fair market value.

"You can bet your ass," Howard said, "they won't pay any fourteen million euros. They'll check the original price, tack on something for inflation and improvements, and offer a couple of million at most."

That was better than having the Camorra make an offer it believed Gore couldn't refuse. A few front men from Naples had already sniffed around. With his habitual penchant for conspiratorial thinking, he claimed, "Some crooks want to grab the villa for themselves. But they'll find out I'm not easy to scare."

Howard laughed. "Jesus, Gore, you sound like somebody from your script—that one you did for Michael Cimino."

The Sicilian. He called the screenplay, based on Mario Puzo's novel, "another impossible effort on my part to turn a hood into Robin Hood."

Later in 1999, Fred Kaplan's *Gore Vidal: A Biography* was released. Contractually, Gore had granted Kaplan access to his papers and personal diaries, promising that he wouldn't read the book before it was published. With that kind of independence Kaplan seemed perfectly positioned to write an authoritative account of a life that, although lived in the public eye, was largely unknown and ill-understood even after *Palimpsest*.

Instead, the biography disappointed its subject so deeply he announced that he had chosen Fred Kaplan in the erroneous belief that he was a different, more prominent author with the same last name. But Jay Parini, a friend who had acted as the middleman between Vidal and Kaplan, sent a letter to *The New York Times*, pointing out that Gore had been under no misapprehension about Fred Kaplan's identity. After the debacle with Walter Clemons, it made sense that Vidal wouldn't authorize a second biography without exercising due diligence. And it was inconceivable that Kaplan, well aware of Gore's reputation for prickliness, would have undertaken the project under false pretenses.

Whatever else might be said about it, the biography, weighing in at more than eight hundred pages, contains a prodigious amount of basic information. Future biographers will inevitably have to consult its exhaustive—and sometimes exhausting—recapitulation of William F. Buckley's libel suit, of Vidal's litigation against Truman Capote, of several dustups with Norman Mailer, and of disputes with various editors and the Screen Writers' Guild. Although Kaplan doesn't often poke fun at Gore, he does characterize *Palimpsest* as "a nonintrospective memoir without a center of consciousness," and he chides its author for imagining he was "stalked by the FBI, the IRS, and the Watergate plumbers" during the short, unsuccessful run of his play *An Evening with Richard Nixon*.

He also includes a few damning quotations from Gore's contemporaries. One from the composer Ned Rorem's diary observes, "I'm sympathetic to virtually everything *chez lui* except the cynical stance. Those steely epigrams summing up all subjects resemble the bars of a cage through which he peers defensively . . . Rather than risk being called a softy, he affects a pose of weariness."

More substantively, Kaplan calls into question Gore's constant complaint that *The City and the Pillar*, with its nonjudgmental depiction of homosexuality, killed his critical and commercial reputation and reduced him to writing pseudonymous mysteries and television screenplays. While it's true that the daily *New York Times* ignored his next half a dozen novels, the Sunday *Times* not only reviewed them but ran an interview with Gore and asked him to write for it. As Kaplan notes, the market for serious fiction was going soft for most novelists, regardless of sexual orientation, and many prominent post–World War II authors depended on college teaching to keep them afloat.

But on the matter of the ultimate faith-based parable in the gospel according to Gore—the hymn of Jimmie Trimble—Kaplan proceeded with caution. He granted that some of Trimble's family and friends in Washington, D.C., expressed displeasure when the story first broke in *Vanity Fair*. Jimmie's mother, Ruth Sewell, then age ninety, and his childhood friend Barrett Prettyman accused Gore of outing a man who had been dead for more than half a century and couldn't defend himself. "If it were true," Kaplan paraphrased their objections, "why had [Vidal] not proclaimed it before?" To which he offered an inadequate answer: "They were unaware that he had done so indirectly in *The City and the Pillar* and *The Season of Comfort*."

Kaplan knew the difference, however, between "indirectly" in fiction and explicitly in nonfiction, and he should not have underestimated Barrett Prettyman as a source, describing him only as a collector of rare first editions and as trustee at St. Albans and the Folger Library. In fact, Prettyman had been a special assistant to Attorney General Robert Kennedy and later an aide to Presidents John Kennedy and Lyndon Johnson. And as a benefactor of Katherine Anne Porter and Richard Yates, Prettyman was no novice in the literary world and was unlikely to object to anything out of mere prudery.

While Gore portrayed his meeting with Jimmie's mother in

Palimpsest as a cordial encounter, Kaplan gingerly corrects the record. "It was a tense, unpleasant few hours." He concedes that the St. Albans teacher who arranged the lunch where Gore asked Mrs. Sewell for copies of Jimmie's letters and a few photographs "was distressed . . . when *Palimpsest* was published." But he leaves unchallenged Gore's speculation that Jimmie Trimble had been sexually molested by his stepfather and that his mother sent him to board at St. Albans to protect him from her husband. Kaplan doesn't comment on Gore's wild surmise that Jimmie had gone on to have other same-sex experiences in the military. Gore's evidence? Jimmie asked his mother to send him Walt Whitman's *Leaves of Grass*. By that logic, readers of Vidal's books might all be suspected of sexual deviance—a suspicion that many a right-wing troglodyte held to be true.

Perhaps for fear of offending Gore, Kaplan appears never to have asked anyone point-blank whether he or she believed the story about Jimmie Trimble. Ultimately, it would come out that many of Vidal's closest friends and family members had their doubts. His half sister Nini said flatly, "Gore and Jimmie didn't happen . . . They didn't have sex."

Offering more background on Jimmie Trimble, *Hardball on the Hill: Baseball Stories from Our Nation's Capital*, by James C. Roberts, concentrates on his athletic exploits but also describes his love for Christine White, the fiancée he left behind when he shipped out to the Pacific. White, who went on to a successful film career and could have been, but wasn't, interviewed by Kaplan—she lived until 2013—corresponded with Jimmie until his death, and there was nothing in his love letters that faintly suggested he led a double life. After Gore claimed in *Vanity Fair* that he and Jimmie had had sex, White wrote the magazine a stinging rebuke, maintaining among other things that Jimmie had never once mentioned Vidal.

Given his accommodating manner, Fred Kaplan must have been aggrieved when Gore reacted angrily to what he regarded as the biographer's excessive interest in his sex life. For more than half a century, Vidal had been a lightning rod in international discussions about homosexuality. Whenever the debate looked as if it might switch away from him, he reinserted himself into the conversation, boasting that no less an authority than Alfred Kinsey had lauded him for his "work in the field" and recorded his sexual history. Kinsey's conclusion, according to Gore, was that he wasn't "homosexual—doubtless because I had never sucked a cock or got fucked."

Supposedly, Kinsey marveled over Vidal's complete lack of guilt about sex. "I told him it was probably a matter of class. As far as I can tell, none of my family ever suffered from that sort of guilt, a middle-class disorder from which power people seem exempt."

Under the circumstances, especially considering that Gore had already violated his own privacy many times over, close scrutiny of his sexuality would seem to have been one of his biographer's principal responsibilities. Such a study might have revealed as much about his books as about his life. But Kaplan chose to err on the side of discretion. There's no evidence that he made any effort to track down any of Gore's thousands of male partners. Instead, he paraphrased Gore's recollections of one-night stands and a few longer affairs. In some instances, he synopsized Vidal's fictionalization of these affairs as if scenes in novels carried the same weight as fact.

As for the women Gore allegedly slept with, Kaplan quoted Rosalind Rust, his high school girlfriend, aged sixteen, as boasting to a friend that Gore was "the best man I ever had in bed." (Years later, in an interview, Kaplan conceded he found no evidence that Gore and Rosalind had had sex.) He noted that Anaïs Nin, a woman of vaster experience and more exacting standards, had disparaged Gore's sexual performance in her journals. And he interviewed Elaine Dundy, Kenneth Tynan's ex-wife, who admitted she had intercourse with Vidal one drunken night. But Kaplan shied away from follow-up questions. Was Gore as indifferent to his partners' pleasure, as a "lousy lay," as he said he was? To what extent was he the bisexual he claimed to be?

These questions weren't addressed, much less answered, until a year after Gore's death, when the British journalist Tim Teeman published a paperback original, *In Bed with Gore Vidal: Hustlers, Hollywood, and the Private World of an American Master*. Despite the book's sensational title, it provides an analysis of "the contradictions and mysteries around [Vidal's] sex life." It also contains a great deal of material about his relations with his family, although it sometimes doesn't subject this information to appropriate double-checking. There is, for example, his half sister's claim, appalling if true, that Gore lived in fear of being exposed as a pedophile. I can only say that in all the years I knew him, I never saw him with an underage sex partner. Nor did I ever hear him in his long history of pungent self-exposure express an interest in children or adolescents as objects of desire.

While Kaplan doesn't mention the daughter Gore sometimes maintained he had as a result of a heterosexual fling, he does deal with a rumor still current around Key West. In the early 1950s, Gore was involved with a woman who demanded that he send her money for an abortion. He did as instructed, and to this day tales circulate on the island about the abortionist's grotesque penchant for displaying the fetus at parties. Kaplan writes that it was hung on a Christmas tree. Sources in Key West say it was used as a decorative Yule log.

By the time Kaplan started his research, Vidal, in his late sixties, lamented that his libido had diminished and he could no longer depend on street boys. He needed "technicians." Because he suffered from high blood pressure and had been prescribed beta-blockers, he was a prime candidate for sexual dysfunction. This must have influenced his mood and his writing, and the fact that he confessed to near impotence for the last thirty years of his life surely had biographical significance. But one would never know this from Kaplan—nor from Gore's memoirs, for that matter.

His daily intake of alcohol undoubtedly contributed to his sexual doldrums. Kaplan took a circumspect approach to this topic as well, either unaware of the chasm he skated over or loath to explore it. "By the 1980s," Kaplan conceded, Gore "had become by most people's standards a heavy drinker." But Kaplan downplayed this, describing his "high tolerance" for alcohol and concluding that "amounts that drove most others under the table found him not only sitting upright but, except for an occasional slurring, absolutely lucid."

Even if this were true, Kaplan ignored the fact that alcoholics often brag that they can go on drinking long after everybody else has passed out. Indeed, the denial of their dependence, along with tales about their greater tolerance, is a recognized symptom of addiction. In any event, Vidal wasn't a secret tippler. For decades he had been a falling-down drunk. If Kaplan hadn't witnessed such episodes, there were plenty of people who could have supplied him with examples.

In a letter, Gore confessed that he liked to "sink myself into whiskey where one's sense of time is so altered that one feels in the moment immortality—a long luminous present which, not drinking, becomes a fast-moving express train named . . . Nothing." As always, he wrote like an angel, even as he hinted at the hellish fear that all that stood between him and oblivion was the bottle.

Gore, in my observation, was agonizingly aware of oblivion. Kaplan didn't see it that way. On the penultimate page of the biography, he repeated Gore's placid summing up, "My makeup is rather cheerful . . . Why would I be depressed about anything?"

THIRTEEN

For a decade after Linda and I left Rome, we felt during visits there that the place was haunted by the shades of old friends. Only Donald and Luisa Stewart and Joan Geller remained of our crowd. Even Mickey Knox, the honorary mayor, had moved his meatless, beanless chili parties to Los Angeles.

Of course, there must have been new prisoners of love that the city held captive. But I preferred to imagine Rome as aging gracelessly, locked in lonely reduced circumstances. I gloated and congratulated myself for jumping ship before twenty-seven McDonald's franchises opened, before a Foot Locker franchise temporarily set up shop on Via Condotti across from Gucci, before the bizarre fad for Irish pubs, before the American Academy ripped out its tennis court, replacing it with a bland greensward called the Mercedes and Sid R. Bass Garden.

But as the calendar ticked over into a new century and Sean and Marc flew the coop, Linda and I decided to spend an autumn in Rome. From the start, we had to concede that for a lady rumored to be on her last legs, the city looked remarkably spry and appealing. Celebrated monuments that had long been webbed with scaffolding and tented under tarpaulin now had their wraps off. Shuttered museums had reopened, and formerly soot-covered facades by Bernini and Borromini were clean and burnished by golden light. Coupling the aesthetic with the practical, many piazzas had been put off-limits to motorized traffic, and pedestrians had less fear of getting run over.

With the advent of the Internet and cell phones, Rome was no longer hostage to its sclerotic postal and landline services. Satellite TV brought in news from the States and European and Middle Eastern nations, and the complexion of the population changed as immigrants swept north from Africa and west from Asia, reducing Rome's provincialism. On Sundays famous basilicas rang out with Abyssinian drummers, Nigerian chants, Korean caroling, sermons in Tagalog, and the impassioned prayers of charismatic Christians who worshipped in the church behind the ancient columns at Portico d'Ottavia.

It didn't take long for us to fall in love with Rome again, and we resumed living there for several months every autumn. Although we had hoped to see more of Howard and Gore, they spent most of the time in Ravello, and reports from La Rondinaia were worrisome. The villa still hadn't sold, and Howard's health had taken a catastrophic turn. Surgeons discovered a tumor in one of his lungs but hesitated to operate because his other, badly compromised lung couldn't sustain him alone.

Then Howard had to be hospitalized for acute abdominal pain. At first, doctors feared he had colon cancer. While they were testing for that, his appendix burst, and he barely survived peritonitis.

Here, the chronology of his medical afflictions became confusing, as did the prognosis. Sometime after his recovery from peritonitis, Howard checked into Cedars-Sinai in Los Angeles for more tests, followed by an operation for the removal of a malignant lung tumor. The surgery was said to have been a success in the sense that Howard was now clear of cancer cells, but there was no assurance that they wouldn't recur.

Back in Ravello, Howard collapsed while climbing out of the pool and wound up in Naples for yet another battery of tests. These revealed that the cancer had metastasized to his brain. Gore attempted to book an immediate flight to Los Angeles but discovered that a commercial plane's "cabin pressure, at transatlantic altitude, would cause the water gathering in [Howard's] skull literally to explode."

Much of this information reached me in London via long-distance calls from Donald and Luisa Stewart. They reported that Gore had moved Howard from Naples to a private clinic in Rome where he was due to undergo an MRI. For decades the two of them had jokingly compared living in Italy to Gauguin's going native on Tahiti. Often they spoke of friends hitting the skids because of their refusal to face reality and repatriate to the States. Now Howard must have felt as miserably trapped as the artist dying in paradise.

When Linda and I arrived for our annual stay in Rome, I had lunch with Gore, hoping for a firsthand report on Howard's health. Gore had checked into the Hotel d'Inghilterra, in the hectic grid of streets at the foot of the Spanish Steps, where each shopwindow is a gilded cage of pricey designer goods—silk scarves, cashmere sweaters, bespoke suits, all with lyrical labels dripping vowels.

He was in the bar, clutching a cane. He told me he needed an operation on his arthritic knee but intended to have it done in the United States, not Italy. He had also herniated a disk helping Howard up after a fall and he shuffled in a painful hunch.

Still, he fizzed with nervous agitation, skittering from subject to subject, gabbling about President Bush and the casus belli that neocon Republicans were building for an invasion of Iraq. He had churned out articles, whole books, about America's campaign against terror and its imperialistic agenda. Then, too, he kept several lawsuits on the boil, some on the back burner, others front and center. Or maybe these were just threats of litigation. It was hard to tell from his disjointed talk.

Obsessing about other subjects to avoid discussing Howard, he started in on Woody Allen, who was in town scouting locations for a film. He and Gore had spent the previous night discussing the vicissitudes of celebrity.

"I thought you didn't like Woody Allen," I broke in.

Gore shrugged.

"I thought you resented him for stealing the premise of *The Purple Rose of Cairo* from *Myron*."

Again he shrugged. Whether out of mellowness or amnesia, he seemed to have reached an armistice with Allen.

We agreed to have dinner that night at Mario's, a restaurant just around the corner. Tottering between Linda and me, Gore wincingly negotiated the cobblestones on Via della Vite. I had booked a table in a back room, and by chance friends of ours, an Italian diplomat and his American wife, were at the adjoining table. With them was Richard Posner, the prominent American economist and judge on the U.S. Court of Appeals for the Seventh Circuit in Chicago.

At Gore's urging, our two groups joined forces. But once we were together, he paid no more than cursory attention to the conversation. Posner had provocative opinions about everything from the legalization of marijuana to the notion that a free market for buying and selling children might be preferable to current adoption laws. He was the sort of formidably brilliant adversary Gore enjoyed jousting with. But not tonight.

Afterward, as Linda and I, each at an elbow, helped him back to the hotel, Gore told us that Howard's MRI had revealed a small, dark bubble on a lobe of his brain. Howard needed immediate surgery, but because Italy was about to shut down on November 1 for Tutti i Santi, it was anybody's guess whether doctors would operate.

Gore entreated us to join him for a nightcap at the Inghilterra. We tried to beg off, pleading fatigue. He said he was tired, too, but knew he wouldn't sleep and didn't want to be alone. "No matter how much I drink, I never get drunk. But some nights liquor lets me nod off for an hour or two."

We sat with him until the early hours, attended by a single surly bartender half-dead on his feet. Gore started in again about Bush and Iraq and Woody Allen, his voice like a recorded announcement broadcasting the same message at intervals.

In the end, the doctor did operate over the All Saints' holiday, after which Howard couldn't walk and suffered hallucinations. Gore hired a private hospital plane to fly them to the States, hopscotching to the Azores, then to Iceland and Indianapolis and finally L.A. He described this horrendous trip as like traveling in "a flying coffin with two nurses, two pilots, Howard, a general assistant from Los Angeles, and me, crippled leg bent under me."

I waited a week, a month. No one in Rome had heard news. Finally, I called the house in Los Angeles and was stunned that Howard answered in his familiar fashion, in a gruff voice that made me fear he might mutter the put-down he favored when bored. "I bet you'd be interested that a friend of mine's sister works for the phone company."

"How are you?" I asked.

"Oh, I'm fine," he said. "I'm dying. That's all. Life goes by quick. Just last night, when we met, we were both so young." It sounded like a line from one of the torch songs he used to croon a cappella at dinner parties. Had brain lesions or medications left him addled?

"Do you want to speak to Gore?" he asked. "Because if you do, he's not here. Maybe you want to talk to my nurse."

"No, I called to say hello to you, Howard."

"And hello to you, too, Mike," he said and hung up.

Howard Austen, aged seventy-four, died of brain cancer in Los Angeles on September 22, 2003. For much of the world his passing made no impression. The news reached me days later when I happened to call La Rondinaia and the housekeeper said Howard had passed away the previous week. I spread word to the few friends of his who had hung on in Rome.

But in California his death was a signal event. Steve Wasserman, the editor of the *Los Angeles Times Book Review*, composed a tribute that placed him in the pantheon of "Enablers of Our Great Creators" and observed how dramatically gender roles had changed since the days when gay writers weren't deemed worthy of inclusion in the literary pantheon and their partners were non-people.

"Behind every great man, it is said, stands a great woman . . . Sometimes the woman is a man," Wasserman wrote. "For Somerset Maugham, it was Alan Searle. For W. H. Auden, it was Chester Kallman. For Christopher Isherwood, it was Don Bachardy. For Gore Vidal, it was Howard Austen."

Lauding Howard's "commitment to the quotidian, to the mundane, to the heroism of everyday life," Wasserman pointed out that "Austen played an invaluable role in making possible the career of a remarkable writer. It was an honorable trade. He was not alone; the tradition of such backstage work is long, if too little recognized . . . These are the men and women who manage the money, make sure the household functions, act as first readers and critics, and in so doing help to free their creative partners from being held hostage to the otherwise grinding reality of daily life. Alas, no Nobels are awarded for such contributions to the republic of letters."

In a testimonial to an entertaining man who had spent his life serving an even more amusing man, Wasserman's piece ended with an anecdote:

> It is said that, from time to time over the decades, Austen, sitting either in their home on Outpost Drive in Hollywood or in their palazzo in Ravello, would, with a sweep of his arm indicating the art hanging on the walls and the

various possessions gathered over a lifetime of travel and collecting, say (with a mischievous gleam in his eye): "You know, Gore, after you're gone, all this will be mine." On one occasion, Vidal, not missing a beat, is said to have replied: "Yes, Howard, that's true, but no one will call." Now, the Great Gore sits alone, the phone ringing, but Howard is no longer there to answer for him.

FOURTEEN

Answering the telephone was the least of what Howard did for Vidal. In addition to handling hundreds of mundane chores, he had monitored Gore's drinking, curbed his excesses, scolded him when he crossed the line, and generally prevented him from plunging over the edge. He hadn't just enabled Gore to create; he had enabled him to continue living when he declared that he wanted to die.

What would happen now? This was the question that filled Gore's friends with foreboding, especially those of us who depended on phone calls to keep in touch. And these calls had to be carefully timed. Because Los Angeles lagged nine hours behind Italy, I rang before dinner from Rome and hoped to catch him not long after he got out of bed.

In winter, when I lived in Key West, the three-hour time difference between Florida and California gave me greater leeway to dial his number, but regardless of the hour he sounded reedy, repetitious, harping on old grievances and new disputes. With less and less interest in fiction, he wrote political screeds about American militarism and constitutional violations. But the more he spoke out, the less the world seemed to listen. As the wars in Iraq and Afghanistan dragged on, he accused the press of taking dictation from the Bush administration. His sense of being marginalized led him to strident statements that, in turn, left him further out on a rhetorical limb, vulnerable to accusations of Lear-like ranting.

Earlier in his career Gore had embodied Marshall McLuhan's concept of a "cool" personality, someone perfect for TV, unflappable under attack, all the more persuasive because he never appeared to be pushing his ideas down the audience's throat. But as he aged, he became a "hot" personality, too impatient to win converts by the power of suggestion, a scold instead of a charmer, an infighter rather than a detached commentator. Where most public performers who hope to continue to play a part in the national conversation accept a reduced role as a lovable old fart or fascinating curmudgeon, Gore insisted on behaving as if he were still the main show, still an enfant terrible deserving of the spotlight. That's a tough sell for a man approaching eighty, rolling downhill in a wheelchair.

For Christmas 2004, Linda and I flew to Los Angeles to visit our son Sean, "the Dwarf," now nearly thirty years old and fully grown at six feet six. He and his fiancée, Desi Van Til, worked in the movie business; Sean had directed several short films, and Desi was an assistant producer at Revolution Studios. When Vidal invited Linda and me to Outpost Drive, they asked to come along to discuss making a movie of his novel *Messiah*.

Twenty-five years had passed since I had seen the house that Gore always likened to the setting for a Raymond Chandler noir. The white-stucco walls and red-tile roofs dating from 1929 had changed very little, and the interior still featured the sort of florid decor for which the term "rococo" had been invented. The living room was the same cavalcade of chinoiserie, golden brocade, and velvet balloon shades. But a huge baroque oil painting by Paolo de Matteis now festooned the ceiling. Vidal said, "There was no space for it elsewhere in the house." One of the scantily clad women in the painting, he deadpanned, was "Princess Margaret asking for another gin and tonic."

Ceremoniously seated in a wheelchair, Gore resembled a Middle Eastern potentate, the dyspeptic master of all he surveyed. Within arm's reach was a George W. Bush doll—a gift from Paul Newman that parroted the forty-third president's most fatuous malapropisms. Hooked over the back of the wheelchair was a cane. Fitted into a holder on one arm of the chair was a tumbler of scotch that Gore sipped at and refilled for the next few hours. He explained that he could walk but preferred not to. "It's great for flying. They wheel you through security right up to the plane."

"But wouldn't the exercise be good for you?" Linda asked.

"Good for what?"

Good for his heart. Good for his spirits. Good for losing weight and relieving some of the pressure on his bad knee. But he couldn't be bothered with any of that. He left the wheelchair just once that evening, to step outside the French doors and pee on the shrubbery.

Later, Sean asked to use the toilet, and Gore insisted that he pee in the backyard, too. Meanwhile, Desi told him how much she admired *Messiah*. Who owned the rights? Could they speak to his agent?

Gore volunteered a few names and his blessing. He believed the novel could make a fine movie. So had the producers of *Hair*, who had flirted with the project. He maintained that *Messiah* had as much box-office potential as *Kalki*. Mick Jagger had optioned the rights to that novel, but it came to nothing. "So many things do," he said, "come to nothing."

La Rondinaia had been on the market for almost five years, and when I asked if there had been any offers, Gore muttered, "More like threats." But reassuring us that the villa didn't just attract lowlifes, he said the queen of Denmark and Ralph Lauren had debated buying it, as had Bruce Springsteen. The inaccessibility of the place, the impossibility of reaching it by car, continued to be a problem, especially because the commune denied permission for a private helicopter pad.

Linda wondered how he liked living in Los Angeles, and Gore said that he was invited to all the best parties, including those thrown by Betsy Bloomingdale, the widow of one of Ronald Reagan's wealthiest supporters. What's more, he was paired off with Nancy Reagan, whom he described as funny, smart, and excellent company. She enjoyed sitting next to him because he could tell her about all the top people in Washington whom he knew and she had never met during her eight years in the White House.

Apparently, she had forgiven the unflattering things he had written about Ronnie and about her nose job and her brief career as an actress who paid suspicious daily visits to a movie mogul's office. And Gore had apparently gotten over his anger at being blackballed from the reception that Ambassador Rabb had thrown for Nancy in Rome.

It was tempting to conclude that ripeness was all and that Vidal had mellowed into a state of sweet acceptance. But when Linda remarked that he appeared to be enjoying life in the United States, he turned snappish. "I would like nothing more than to lead a revolution of rebels from Canada."

That, in a nutshell, defined his contradictory character. He was a man who treasured evenings with Betsy Bloomingdale and Nancy Reagan—and wanted to eradicate all they represented.

As he steadily drank, Gore repeated a story about one of his caregivers who was sexually attracted to Swedish women because of their smell. He dismissed this as idiotic romanticism, pheromonal hogwash, utterly at odds with his own erotic urges, which he described for Desi and Sean's benefit. "I just like to get it up, get off, and hurry to get it up again."

From sexual swashbuckling he segued to the subject of his enduring popularity. Why, he wondered, did crowds stream into amphitheaters and college auditoriums to hear him speak? Why did young people line up to shake his hand and beg him to sign their books?

"Because of your great modesty," Linda suggested.

Gore laughed at himself but soon began gesturing angrily at a photograph of Howard on a sideboard. Working himself into a lather, he lamented that this wasn't how it was supposed to be. He was supposed to die before Howard. "Look at him there holding his suicide weapon."

In the photograph, Howard held an umbrella. For an instant I was puzzled. Then I noticed the cigarette between his fingers. "Smoking was what killed him. He might as well have used a razor blade," Gore said, clinging to his own suicide weapon, a tumbler of scotch.

In clinical detail he described Howard's death, recalling his friend's eyes and their "evolution or devolution." Once he stopped breathing, his pupils no longer moved, and Gore knew "he no longer inhabited the husk of his body." Even so, a CPR emergency team "heaved Howard around on the floor trying to restart his heart. Vitreous fluid flowed from his eyes like yolk from a cracked egg."

By now it was dark, long past dinnertime in early-to-bed L.A. Not that he showed any interest in eating. Nor did he give any indication that he meant to offer us food. Only alcohol was available in abundance, alcohol and an all-pervasive pain. He told us that he often listened to CDs of Howard singing American standards. He confessed that he sometimes cried.

"I'm doing another memoir," he said. "This one follows my life from age thirty-nine till today."

That we had just listened to a central chapter of it I had no doubt. And if he wrote the scene as well as he had recounted it, no one, I thought, could possibly believe Gore was as icily remote as he was accused of being.

At the conclusion of *Palimpsest* Gore had observed, "I seem to have written, for the first and last time, not the ghost story that I feared but a love story." With *Point to Point Navigation*, published in 2006, he spun another love story, this one with Howard supplanting Jimmie Trimble as the object of his adoration. Indeed Trimble was barely mentioned, and when asked by an interviewer for *The Times* of London whether Jimmie had been the love of his life, Gore admitted, "That was a slight exaggeration. I said it because there wasn't any other."

In death, Howard had become more significant to him than he ever was when alive. He had even infiltrated Gore's dreams. "We were in a side street in Rome," he wrote, "where the entrance to our old flat should have been but was nowhere to be found." It was an eerie reminder of that night after dinner at Passetto when Gore was too fuddled by vodka to find the door to his apartment.

Retroactively, he declared in *Point to Point Navigation* that concern about Howard's health had shaped his decisions for decades. The home on Outpost Drive, he wrote, was never intended as a bolt-hole during the Red Brigades era nor as an alternate residence to evade Italian taxes. Instead, long before Howard fell ill, he "bought the house in Los Angeles . . . to prepare for the hospital years which came even sooner than either suspected."

Later, in *Snapshots in History's Glare*, he insisted that the purchase of La Rondinaia in 1972 had also been spurred by fears that Howard's emphysema would metastasize into brain cancer. So thirty years in advance, he provided Howard "as pleasant a last stand as I could have made for him."

Was his memory failing? Was he losing his grip on the narrative of his life? Or in his grief was he indulging in magical thinking, revising the past as he wished it had been?

Like *Palimpsest*, which started off with a definition of its title, *Point to Point Navigation* opened with a note clarifying this nautical term. But it proved to be an inapposite metaphor for his second memoir's wayward course through the shoals of memory. Seemingly lost at sea, Gore latched onto rehashed vignettes as if they were life preservers. The early chapters were a reprise of *Screening History*, his book about the impact of movies on his life. Inevitably, he cited his cameo role in *Fellini's Roma* and added that the film was released in 1972. Neither he nor a copy editor noticed that on the previous page a photograph carried a caption, "It is 1973 and I am playing myself in *Fellini's Roma*."

As he chronicled his life in Italy, he again failed to mention Mickey Knox, Donald and Luisa Stewart, Steve and Joan Geller, or even George Armstrong, although he was then sending money to his old cruising companion, who was hard up in the States. Yet he included a troublingly Capote-esque anecdote about an evening in Russia with Graham Greene, who, Gore wrote, "was particularly exciting on the subject of Castro, with whom he had fought side by side in Oriente Province during the revolution. I could not tell if he was making it up as he went along or whether or not he was actually calling upon memory."

The same question might have been asked of him. Was he making it up? Perhaps at that point Gore couldn't have said himself. Or with glee had he realized that people were prepared to believe almost anything without checking the facts? Why should he bother to write the truth when everybody got it wrong anyway?

Yet there were times when he still felt afflicted by lies and sailed forth like Captain Ahab hell-bent on harpooning the white whale. In the summer of 2007 the *London Review of Books* reprinted Truman Capote's libel that a drunken Gore Vidal had been bodily heaved from the White House by Bobby Kennedy. Gore requested—no, he demanded—my help. He instructed me to contact the *LRB* and threaten that if it didn't publish a retraction and an apology, he would sue and ruin it financially.

You may call me Ishmael. You may call me a fair-weather

friend. But I would never have become involved in this imbroglio if I hadn't at the same time been charged by the Key West Literary Seminar with persuading Gore to speak at a conference on historical fiction. His eminence in the genre made him a natural choice, as did his connection to Tennessee Williams and his popularity with the island's gay community. While I wouldn't describe the invitation as a capstone to his career, it was an opportunity for people who cared about him to pay homage. Donald and Luisa Stewart planned to fly in from Rome for the festivities, as did Gore's friend and literary executor, Jay Parini.

But he refused to discuss the Literary Seminar while his blood was boiling about the *London Review of Books*. When I recommended that he hire a barrister, he asked why he should waste thousands of pounds when he had me on the scene in London. It wouldn't take ten minutes, he said. The *LRB* didn't have a legal leg to stand on.

When I continued to demur, he frostily replied, "You want me, a man in a wheelchair, to fly across the country to speak at your charming little Chautauqua. Yet when all I ask is that you make a phone call . . ."

I capitulated.

British libel law, unlike its American cousin, is punitively reductive. Neither the writer nor the publisher has recourse to the kinds of defenses that complicate matters in U.S. courts. Public figures don't have to prove reckless or malicious disregard for the truth, and they can, if the facts are in their favor, rest assured that the losing party must pick up all legal costs.

In a case such as *Vidal v. Capote*, where prime facie libel had been proven decades earlier, the *London Review of Books* faced disastrous consequences. So I assumed the magazine would be grateful that Vidal wasn't demanding monetary damages. I also assumed that Inigo Thomas, the author of the article, wouldn't object to setting the record straight.

But I assumed wrong and came to recognize how often Gore

must have suffered the same maddening runaround I experienced. If he was cantankerous and confrontational, it might have had something to do with the smugness of the opposition ranged against him. When I rang the *London Review of Books*, I got bounced from department to department, person to person, each of whom listened with palpable indifference to Vidal's complaint. This was, they gave me to understand, just another hysterical outburst by a famously tetchy author.

Yes, I agreed, a famously tetchy author who was also famously rich and litigious and determined to get satisfaction. What possible objection could they have against informing readers that as a matter of proven fact Gore hadn't been bodily thrown out of the White House by Bobby Kennedy? Would the *London Review of Books* prefer to pay hundreds of thousands of pounds in damages and legal costs? The right course for everybody involved was to settle things amicably.

Instead, *LRB* chose to publish a letter from Inigo Thomas that muddied the issue. Rather than conceding that he had been wrong to repeat Truman Capote's libel, Thomas wrote, "In my article about Gore Vidal, I should have made it clear that there are different versions of Vidal's evening at the White House in November 1961 and the confrontation that took place there."

As if he needed to do no more than balance conflicting accounts, Thomas summarized Vidal's side of the story. He conceded that Capote had "maliciously embellished a different story" but ended with a comment that inflamed Gore almost as much as Capote's original libel. "There seems little reason to think that this episode isn't an example of Vidal's hatred of being told what he can and can't do, even or especially by the second most important man in the Kennedy White House."

Gore was apoplectic. Somehow what was supposed to have been an apology had soured into another depiction of him as a prima donna driven by egotistical pique.

"Call them back," Gore said, "and tell them that unless they run a retraction in the next issue, I intend to take them to court. Tell them I'll end up owning the magazine and having the pleasure of firing every one of them."

On July 19, 2007, the *London Review of Books* printed an apology:

> In his review of Gore Vidal's *Point to Point Navigation*, Inigo Thomas unintentionally repeated an allegation first made by Truman Capote: that Gore Vidal got drunk while on a visit to the White House during the Kennedy era. In fact, the story is untrue. We are happy to say we are sorry, to set the record straight by making it clear that Vidal did not get drunk as claimed, and to point out that he sued Capote successfully for making this allegation many years ago. A true account of the incident is given in Vidal's autobiography *Palimpsest*.

FIFTEEN

After that, Gore committed to speak at the 2009 Key West Literary Seminar. "If I'm still alive, I'll be there," was the way he put it. For the next eighteen months he and the seminar's board exchanged brusque messages concerning the terms of his appearance, and to my distress many of these messages sizzled like loose live wires through me.

The board members needed some idea of what he intended to talk about. It wasn't enough for him to maintain that his topic was always the same: America, its history, mores, and duplicity. They needed a title, not to mention biographical information, for their advertising brochure. In a late-night phone call to London, the seminar's executive director, Miles Frieden, lamented to me that his efforts to discuss matters with Gore had smacked into a brick wall. "Since he won't talk to me," Frieden said, "could you deal with him?"

I timed my transatlantic calls to reach him in L.A. in mid-afternoon, which meant midnight London time. Because of my fatigue I probably sounded as foggy as he did. But the fits and stutters of his responses were, I feared, permanent conditions, the up-shot of what Tennessee Williams used to refer to as insults to the brain. Through Donald and Luisa Stewart, I learned that Gore had recently flown to India for a literary conference. When he landed and discovered no welcoming committee, no red carpet rolled out for him, he climbed right back on the plane and returned to Los Angeles. More than vanity, this suggested dementia. But as Gore cheerfully confirmed the story, it also sounded like an admonition to me as we got down to the brass tacks of his talk in Key West. You crossed him at your peril.

While he understood that other authors—Barry Unsworth, Peter Matthiessen, Joyce Carol Oates, Marilynne Robinson, and so on—had signed on to appear at the Literary Seminar, he wanted no part of them or of panel discussions. He expected star billing and top dollar. But after negotiating a handsome honorarium, he turned around and donated it to the seminar, demonstrating again that recognition and status meant more to him than money.

He demanded first-class air travel for himself and two caregivers. Because the small island-skimming planes from Miami to Key West couldn't accommodate his wheelchair, a minivan was dispatched to drive him and his entourage down highway A1A. Housed in ground-floor, wheelchair-accessible rooms at the Marquesa Hotel, the group was welcome to stay as long as it liked.

Gore declined to deliver a formal lecture, so Jay Parini was invited to serve as a moderator. There would be an onstage interview, followed by an open-mike question-and-answer session with the audience.

A professor at Middlebury College, Parini had met Gore by happenstance during a vacation on the Amalfi coast, and the two struck up a friendship. A successful fiction writer, biographer, and filmmaker—the adaptation of his novel *The Last Station* earned Academy Award nominations for Helen Mirren and Christopher Plummer—Parini often accompanied Gore on book tours, and his presence seemed to soothe, or at least restrain, him. This fed my sense of cautious optimism, as did the fact that Gore had so many fans in Key West, all devoted to the idea that the seminar would be a gala celebration of his return to the island, most likely for the last time. In addition to Parini, and Donald and Luisa Stewart, Ann Beattie and her husband, the artist Lincoln Perry, had known Gore for years, and they lived next door to the Marquesa and volunteered to lend a hand.

Then there was David Wolkowsky. Like Gore, he was in his mid-eighties and much admired on the island as a real estate visionary who bought up whole blocks of derelict houses during the 1970s and helped revive Key West as a winter retreat for a clientele that spent summers in the Hamptons or on Martha's Vineyard. More than just a local Midas, he was active in the arts, entertained writers on his private island, Ballast Key, and threw an annual party during the Literary Seminar at his rooftop apartment. Wolkowsky eagerly awaited Gore's arrival, explaining that he had enjoyed meeting him decades earlier through their mutual friend Tennessee Williams.

The schedule kicked off with an art opening, featuring new work by Lincoln Perry. Afterward, there was to be a reception and supper at Tennessee Williams's house. Although Gore voiced disgruntlement that Hemingway's place was a museum, while the Glorious Bird's was privately owned by a Republican businessman, he agreed to attend the event.

By the time I got to the Lucky Street Gallery, Gore was rolling idly amid clumps of guests who eyed him askance and kept their distance. He looked like a down-and-out panhandler who had sneaked in off Duval Street to swipe a drink and a fistful of peanuts. A sad, shrunken doll in a rumpled blue blazer with an antimacassar of dandruff around the shoulders, he wore stained sweatpants and bright white tennis sneakers and sat slumped to one side in his wheelchair, as if the bones had been siphoned out of his body.

Shocked and attempting not to show it, I came over to greet

him. Maybe he was as flabbergasted by my appearance as I was by his. With no polite chitchat, he asked, "Are you still continent?"

I restrained an impulse to check my fly and make sure I wasn't leaking. "I was when I left home."

"Well, I'm not," he declared. "And I could care less."

As people gathered around, a gallery employee arranged an impromptu receiving line. "Here's someone I'm sure you'd like to meet, Mr. Vidal. Joy Williams."

He didn't so much as glance in her direction. "Why would I want to meet Joy Williams?"

She was followed by the Pulitzer Prize–winning novelist Alison Lurie, at whose name Gore growled, "Next."

When Judy Blume paid her respects, he hummed "God Save the Queen."

Meeting Judith Gaddis and learning that she had been married to William Gaddis, Gore called her former husband a cheapskate and said Gaddis had stuck him with a restaurant bill in Rome.

Strangely, no one except me appeared to be appalled by any of this. They laughed, as if they were at a roast at the National Press Club, an hour of insults to inaugurate the Literary Seminar. I was reminded of Jean Genet, who, even after he was rich and world famous, continued to steal. He stole from friends, patrons, publishers, and hosts at parties and claimed that middle-class people expected it. "If I don't steal something from them they're not happy." Perhaps the same held true for Gore; people expected him to be outrageous, and he seldom disappointed them.

When we adjourned to Tennessee Williams's house, Gore was seated on a couch and clamped his capped teeth in a rictus-like grimace calculated to keep interlopers away. But a silver-haired lady bravely slid in beside him and pressed close for a tête-à-tête.

Susan Mesker was a tireless donor to the arts and a major benefactor of the Literary Seminar. She owned eleven houses in

Key West and regularly put them at the disposal of visiting writers. Sober and in a kindlier mood, Gore might have regarded Mrs. Mesker, as he had my father-in-law, as "a bore, but my kind of bore." That night he could abide her for no more than ten minutes before he barked for somebody to "get this drunken cross-eyed cunt out of my face."

As Susan Mesker slunk away, nobody objected, at least not out loud. No one suggested that Gore be dispatched on the next plane to Los Angeles. And later, at David Wolkowsky's rooftop party, nobody did anything except gawk when the host greeted the honored guest, exclaiming, "Gore, what a pleasure to see you after so many years," and Gore glacially replied, "I've never seen you before in my life."

In subsequent days it seemed doubtful that he would be in any shape to speak at the Literary Seminar or that he would be coherent if he did manage to wheel his chair onstage. Sunk deep in dread—unlike the producers at C-SPAN who optimistically planned to televise his talk—I depended on friends to help keep him more or less compos mentis. Ann Beattie and Lincoln Perry manned the morning shift, coaxing him to eat a bite or two of breakfast before he hit the bottle.

Of the two minders who accompanied him from L.A., one was an Eastern European who restricted himself to overseeing Gore's medications. The other, an affable young fellow, Fabian Bouthillette, nicknamed Fabi, had no prior experience as a caregiver. A graduate of the Naval Academy, he had resigned his commission and joined the protest movement Iraq Veterans Against the War. It was as a political activist that he had attracted Gore's attention, and it was Fabi's admiration of Gore's antiwar stance that persuaded him to become an unpaid manservant. Apart from pushing the wheelchair and bundling Gore in and out of cars, Fabi provided a sounding board for his political fulminations. He had no interest in Gore's sexual views. Nor for that matter did Gore, in his feeble haze, indulge in any of his renegade erotic shenanigans. He just wanted to drink.

In Fabi's opinion Gore was displaying symptoms of brain damage, and he wondered why his relatives hadn't intervened and gotten him medical care. Of the many things Gore told him, Fabi reserved judgment about what was fact and what was alcoholic conflation. For example, he didn't accept at face value Gore's claim that he had a daughter. But sometime later in L.A., Fabi, now officially on the payroll, was screening Gore's mail one day and opened an envelope that contained a photograph of a middle-aged woman who bore an uncanny resemblance to him. She wrote that she had reason to believe that he was her biological father. Fabi passed the letter along to Gore, who said nothing about it.

Some mornings Alison Lurie went to the Marquesa to keep Gore company. Although he had urged her to stop by and talk, he struck her as irrationally angry, perhaps in shame at having her see him in such shambles. His sentences, once so crisp and shapely, slithered off into nonsequiturs.

By the time I showed up for my shift after lunch, Donald and Luisa were usually sitting with Gore beside the pool. The food they had ordered for him from room service remained uneaten. Fabi had watered down his scotch, but Gore caught on to that trick and demanded a fresh bottle.

When the talk turned to Rome, he grew wistful and wished he had never left. He vowed in a throbbing voice that he would return. He had bought a house in France in the hills above the Riviera for Muzius Dietzmann, one of his most loyal employees, and Luisa urged him to use it as a base for side trips to Italy.

As for La Rondinaia, he said he had sold it to local investors in Ravello who intended to transform it into a luxurious boutique hotel. By all accounts the buyers drove a hard bargain and got it for 12.4 million euros, nearly $16 million.

He had also managed to sell the first-century A.D. mosaic of the mythological hippocamp. He didn't care to discuss its price; he preferred to brag how the heavy mosaic had had to be removed at the new owner's expense by helicopter. I later learned that the hippocamp had been purchased for 30,000 euros. In 2013, the current owner offered it to me for 160,000 euros but conceded that it could never legally leave Italy.

The bust of Jove that Gore had bought in New York and imported back to Italy was a memento he refused to part with. To get around the embargo on antiquities, he had it covered in wax and identified on the bill of lading as a candleholder. Then he shipped it ahead to Los Angeles, hoodwinking authorities in both countries.

The night of Gore's appearance at the Literary Seminar, a group of us gathered with him in the greenroom. There had been some debate about whether to have a bottle of Glenlivet on hand or whether it was wiser to deny him a last slug of scotch. In the end, he got his bottle and nipped at it as a journalist quizzed him about the Iraq War, Afghanistan, and the state of the Union. On all scores he was resolutely bleak.

Wishing Jay Parini good luck in his role as moderator, I went to join an audience that seemed to share my apprehension. The atmosphere was reminiscent of Old-Timers' Day at a ballpark, where fans applaud aging heroes while praying that they don't embarrass themselves or break their necks.

Advancing into the spotlight in his wheelchair, a cane clamped between his knees, Gore looked like the last survivor of some half-remembered military campaign, wearing a grayish-brown suit and striped peach-colored shirt open at the throat. With his deeply lined face fixed in a grin, he got off to a good start. When Parini reminded him of what he had baptized as the United States of Amnesia, Gore drawled, "I had forgotten that."

But then he maundered on and on about America's having "the worst educational system on earth," which somehow led him to a garrulous discussion of *Family of Secrets*, a book about the Bushes. "A family of criminals," he declared. "If I seem in a daze, it's because I've been reading about their crimes."

Parini tried to prod him back to the seminar's theme, historical fiction. But Gore ignored the cues and veered off on a tangent about FDR, delivered in the president's Brahmin accent. He claimed that FDR, wheelchair-bound like Gore, had once gotten trapped in a bathroom and had to be rescued by a sailor.

Jay asked him to say something—anything!—about Abraham Lincoln. Gore chided Doris Kearns Goodwin—he called her Doris Stern—for borrowing material from his novel for her popular book *Team of Rivals*.

Suddenly, in a crackling synapse, it occurred to him that his cycle of novels known as the Narratives of Empire had skipped the Mexican War. He mused that he might write about that next. "So many lies have been told," he said. But the lies he chose to decry were those he blamed on the Bush administration, not the nineteenth-century American invaders of Mexico.

Parini expressed admiration for *Julian* and inquired how he had happened to write a novel about the last pagan Roman emperor. Gore got his wires crossed and summarized the plot of *Creation*.

When the audience was invited to ask questions, he blundered through his answers, often unable to sustain a thought for the length of a sentence. He offered fragments, scattered phrases, and paraphrases from old essays. Teddy Roosevelt, Alice Roosevelt Longworth, Tennessee Williams, Caroline Kennedy—their names streamed by like eye floaters, dispersing before any point had been made. He struggled to retrieve the title of the book he was reading and had to be prompted by the audience. "*Family of Secrets*," someone shouted. Then he had trouble remembering the names of his own novels. "Not *Julian*, the other one that begins with *J*," he muttered aloud, unable to call to mind *The Judgment of Paris.*

He perked up at a question about Amelia Earhart. "I wanted my father to marry her." He insisted she was as good a poet as she was a pilot. They had read her verses together in the bleachers during the Army-Navy game, which his father, the former football star, had badgered them into attending with him. The anecdote ended with his speculation that Earhart's fatal plane crash in the Pacific had actually been suicide. He said his father had assured him that Amelia was quite capable of murdering her co-pilot while killing herself.

For anyone interested, Gore's performance at the 2009 Key West Literary Seminar is posted on C-SPAN's Web site. I've watched it several times and can't help cringing, just as I did that night. But most people I've spoken to expressed simple gratitude that he got through the event without a complete breakdown.

Afterward, beneath a balmy star-spangled sky, we gathered for a buffet dinner on the grounds of the Key West lighthouse, across the street from Ernest Hemingway's walled compound and its pride of six-toed cats. The table assigned to Gore stood on a stretch of damp grass that sucked at the wheels of his chair and threatened to tip it over. With much huffing and puffing, several of us hauled him, like a bobble-head doll, onto firmer ground.

Whatever people might have made of his performance, he had admirers here, fans of his fiction, political fellow travelers, celebrators of his sexual trailblazing. Some stopped by to shake his hand. Some snapped photographs. Like the well-practiced pol he was, Gore smiled for them all. Even Susan Mesker sat with us for a spell, harboring no apparent ill will. But when Luisa Stewart asked what he would like her to bring him from the buffet, he snarled, "How about a pistol?"

Luisa laughed nervously. "So you can shoot me?"

"No," he said. "So I can shoot myself."

When we were alone, he reached over and touched my hand. "Help me, Mike, I don't know what I'm supposed to feel."

There was so much I might have said. I might have told him that he had left it too late to learn. Or setting aside a fear that I would be mocked, I might have assured him that there was still hope, there was still time to reconnect with all that he had cut himself off from. Instead, I simply held on to his hand, his bones so fragile I was pierced by terrible sadness.

For dramatic effect and narrative concision, I might claim that these were the last words Gore and I exchanged. The truth is in the next couple of days he uttered other words, not all of them coherent, and as I had done so often in the past, I feared every time I left him that I would never see him alive again. Nobody could survive the sort of punishment he inflicted on himself. But somehow he wobbled through the week, and after his departure from Key West he set off on a wide-ranging itinerary that sparked troubling reports in the press. He flew to England and addressed Parliament as if it were a clutch of schoolchildren. At a conference in Istanbul, according to London's *Sunday Times*, he heaped anathema upon the whole nation, condemning Turkey, in its present incarnation, as a country unworthy of its history.

The following year, on a trip to Europe, he appeared to come unstuck altogether. In France with Fabi and Muzius, Gore demanded to be flown back to Los Angeles. When the two were slow, in his opinion, to make airline reservations, he accused them of kidnapping him and phoned his nephew Burr Steers. Somehow he then got it in his head that Burr was colluding with Fabi and Muzius, and by the time he returned to the States, he had alienated almost everybody.

I followed these events from a distance, with updates from Jay Parini and Donald and Luisa Stewart. Gore and I just missed connecting in the South of France and in Rome. Then, while I spent the winter in Key West, he commuted between L.A. and New York, preparing for the revival of his 1960 play, *The Best Man*.

On the Internet, I noticed that his house on Outpost Drive was for sale. "The Mediterranean mini-mansion," once white, now re-stuccoed a shade of ocher, boasted new wrought-iron gates barring the driveway. The asking price—$3,495,000—didn't seem excessive for a five-bedroom, four-bathroom estate in an area where Gore had Charlize Theron, Kyle MacLachlan, and Ben Stiller for neighbors.

I wondered why he was selling. Where did he plan to live? I meant to call and ask him, but I didn't, and more months passed.

In the spring of 2012, I belatedly learned, Gore underwent a brain scan that revealed extensive deterioration and symptoms of Wernicke-Korsakoff syndrome, a condition common to long-term alcoholics. Then, on August 1, I woke in London to the news that he had died the day before at the age of eighty-six at his home in Los Angeles. The cause of death was said to be complications from pneumonia.

Much like Gore that night at the Key West lighthouse, I didn't know what I was supposed to feel. Sad, of course. Resigned. But I was also filled with remorse, just as he had been after Howard's death. For years I had realized that he was killing himself with drink, and I felt helpless at not having been able to stop him.

The international outpouring of obituaries and eulogies would have delighted him, especially those that praised his elegance, aristocratic bearing, mandarin style, and exalted achievements in different genres. He wouldn't even have minded the less-flattering characterizations—"cynical," "acerbic," "misanthropic," "elitist." He had been called worse and wore these pejorative labels like badges of honor.

For *The Washington Post*, I wrote a reminiscence alerting readers that for all the accolades he was currently receiving, he had for much of his career been on the sharp end of bitter rejections. If at times he had acted like a literary Mike Tyson, reveling in behavior befitting the baddest man on the planet, it was because of the pain he had absorbed, beginning with his own family.

People marked his passing in their own fashion. Before he left Italy, Gore had given Donald and Luisa Stewart the cut-glass chandelier that used to hang above the dinner table at La Rondinaia. Now it lit their dining room in Rome, and at every meal they remembered their friend.

In Key West, Arlo Haskell, the associate director of the Literary Seminar, had saved what was left of the bottle of Glenlivet that Gore had nipped at in the greenroom before his talk. Arlo had vowed not to drink it until Vidal died. Now he invited a few friends to join him in polishing off the fifth.

Whenever I was asked what Gore was "really like"—a question that would have set his teeth on edge—I found myself recalling his postmortem remarks about Tennessee Williams: "I suppose too much had been made of his later years when he was often on pills or drunk and not always coherent. But, at his best, he was corrosively funny." That was what I remember about Gore—how funny he was. And how generous and hospitable. Not at all the bitchy, vengeful man his critics imagined.

It was a shame that he never felt adequately appreciated. But perhaps if he had, he wouldn't have accomplished half as much as he did. He embodied Goethe's dictum that "the world only goes forward because of those who oppose it." And those who oppose it have to expect to take their lumps.

Gore often joked that anybody who wasn't paranoid wasn't in full possession of the facts. So he would have chortled knowingly when *The New York Times*, in its end-of-the-year group celebrity obituary, "The Lives They Lived," ignored him while memorializing the writers Nora Ephron, Paul Fussell, Adrienne Rich, and Maurice Sendak. Nothing could have done more to confirm his faith in the

Great Eraser, the conspiratorial force he believed was determined
to eliminate him from the literary map.

Of course, he lives on in his books, in his plays, and in the films
he wrote and the ones he acted in. Then, too, there are his good
works. Quite apart from his generosity to me, he gave more than
can easily be estimated to the nation, and there can only be regret
that he's no longer around to speak out against bumptious big government and predatory big business and to speak on behalf of those
ill-equipped to defend themselves. In the end I feel as Gore wrote
that he did as he watched Eleanor Roosevelt's funeral cortege dis-
appear: "Well, that's that. We're really on our own now."

Epilogue

Three months after Gore's death, there was a memorial service in New York City at the Gerald Schoenfeld Theatre on West Forty-fifth Street, where his play *The Best Man* had been revived. With Dick Cavett acting as emcee, a glittering retinue of acquaintances, literary colleagues, and hangers-on, some of whom he had publicly broken with, gathered to give readings from his work and deliver encomiums. News accounts mentioned no member of his family who might have been in attendance. The spotlight was on Anjelica Huston, Candice Bergen, Elizabeth Ashley, Cybill Shepherd, and Elaine May, all of whom seemed to supply Hollywood's stamp of approval. But this would not prevent Gore from being passed over at the 2013 Academy Awards during the "In Memoriam" segment. His battles with the Screen Writers' Guild had never sat well with the academy.

Because I didn't return to the States until January 2013, I missed the memorial service. But several weeks later on a trip to Los Angeles, I wanted to pay my respects with a visit to his home on Outpost Drive. Calling ahead, I spoke to the housekeeper, Norberto Nierras, who answered the phone with a breezy "Gore Vidal's residence." When I introduced myself, he said, "Mr. Vidal's dead."

"I know. But I hoped I could stop by and—"

"Everything's in the hands of the lawyers. I can do nothing without permission."

"Would it help me to contact his nephew Burr Steers?"

"No. The lawyers are in charge. If they say yes, I'll call you back."

His call never came, and it wasn't until later that I learned of the legal wrangles Gore's will created. Little more than a year before his death, he added a codicil, bequeathing his entire estate, estimated at thirty-seven million dollars, to Harvard University. He left nothing to his half sister Nina Straight or his three other half siblings, nor did he make good on a verbal promise to pass his house along to Burr Steers. The family is challenging the will, on the grounds that Gore was mentally incompetent when he agreed to the codicil.

Although news reports suggested that Vidal had no connection to Harvard and therefore no reason to leave it a fortune, it's worth noting that the university didn't simply represent an illustrious institution whose imprimatur he craved. Harvard had played a direct role in his career ever since the publication of *Lincoln*. Professor David Herbert Donald, an eminence on the history faculty, had vetted *Lincoln* for accuracy and defended it against critics. In 1991, Harvard invited Vidal to deliver the Massey Lectures, and from these grew Gore's book *Screening History*, published by Harvard University Press. After that Gore donated all his papers to Harvard. While he might have been accused of many things, he was unfailingly loyal to those who returned the favor.

In Rome for my annual stay in the fall of 2013, I heard that La Rondinaia, after six years of renovations, remained empty. The current owners had decided to seek new investors, still hoping to open the villa as a luxury hotel and center for conventions and wedding receptions. But as Vincenzo Palumbo, one of the original investors, explained, the need for extensive repairs had stalled their plans. He said Gore had left La Rondinaia in poor condition. The wiring and plumbing had to be updated, and the bare concrete floors covered by hand-laid tiles.

On a warm October afternoon, Palumbo let me make a last pilgrimage to the villa, ushering me down the familiar allée of trees carpeted with the spiny husks of fallen chestnuts. Construction equipment, piles of debris, bags of cement, and black plastic sheeting dotted the property. Palumbo detoured from the path to show me a mosaic that had been removed from La Rondinaia and remounted behind a fountain. He was less eager to linger at the swimming pool, where the water was the color of iced tea and teeming with frogs and fish, some dead and floating like the corpse in Norma Desmond's pool in *Sunset Blvd.*

We ducked under the green pods dangling from a wisteria arbor and swatted our way through cobwebs to a final staircase, now a ramp for wheelbarrows. At the entrance to La Rondinaia, the lichen-stained statue of a lion resembled a leprously spotted cat crouched under drooping electrical lines. Rusty scaffolding spiderwebbed the walls.

I didn't want to go inside. The rattle of Palumbo's key in the front door set off horror-movie harmonics. It was as if we were stepping into a mausoleum instead of a house where I had happily spent weeks. But then visits to the homes of dead writers always fill me with a sense of woe. Like locust shells, they lack everything that previously animated them—the buzz, the voracious appetite, the ambitious flights.

The new mosaic floors, I acknowledge, were a lavish improvement, and the refitted bathrooms—one of them festooned with gold and lapis tiles—were of an opulence that would have dazzled a Venetian doge. But devoid of furniture and all except the most distant memories, the other rooms emphasized Gore's absence more keenly than anything had before. Bare wires bristled on walls; discarded trash lined the corridor; harsh light from uncurtained windows glinted off the whitewash.

Palumbo rashly promised that the place could be put into perfect order in two months—once they had more money. He also promised that Signor Vidal's study would stay as it had been, preserved as a mini-museum. So I followed him into it with the expectation that I would find tangible evidence of my friend. Instead, I entered what looked like a crime scene waiting to be processed by a forensics squad. The table where Gore had written every book beginning with *Burr* was warped and weather-beaten. Rather than the manuscripts and correspondence that once littered it, there was a crazy quilt of objects that suggested the underside of his life. Scattered around a portable typewriter—one of four in the room—lay a leather scabbard for a missing letter opener, a dirty drinking glass, a roll of masking tape, a faded sheaf of curling photographs, a last, irreducible matryoshka doll, half a bottle of scotch, and half a bottle of gin.

In the tufa fireplace, as if awaiting a match, were six sealed boxes of his books translated into French, Spanish, Italian, and Catalan. What a bonfire of the vanities they would have made! On shelves within easy reach of his desk there used to be research volumes that Gore consulted as he wrote. These had been supplanted by copies of his own books, all redolent of mildew and rot. I picked out a paperback of *Williwaw* and one of *The City and the Pillar*, then fled La Rondinaia with snippets of Shelley's "Ozymandias" roiling around in my head.

Though tempted to drive straight back to Rome, I forced myself to slow down and stroll around Ravello. While it had bestowed honorary citizenship on him, the village had always maintained a discreet distance from Vidal. He preferred it that way; it allowed him privacy, which local people respected. Few of them had ever been inside La Rondinaia, and they politely referred to Gore and Howard as "the writer" and "his secretary." Many of them had no idea how famous he was until after his death.

Now Ravello, unlike his vacant villa, was full of him. A massive billboard advertising the town's annual cultural festival featured a three-times life-size color picture of Gore that appeared to leer at Man Ray's famous photograph of Kiki of Montparnasse, her nude back curved like a cello. In shops and restaurants snapshots of him were displayed the way images of JFK adorn Latin American homes. At the bar Al San Domingo a quotation from Vidal is stenciled on the wall behind the cash register:

> Ravello is situated in the most beautiful of all Mediterranean settings, a fact that is not at first apparent. But by the time one has made the circuit from Villa Rufolo to Villa Cimbrone and back to the piazza, the magic has been demonstrated and the Bar San Domingo offers comfort!

Across the piazza in a jewelry shop, Giorgio Filocamo kept a photograph of Gore on the wall along with snapshots of Susan Sarandon and Ben Gazzara. His recollections of Signor Vidal were warm and affectionate but not clouded by sentiment. The sort of philosophical Italian who expresses himself in parables that would sound inconceivable coming from an American shopkeeper, Giorgio recounted how Gore had once arrived with Ambassador and Mrs. Rabb and bought them gifts. He described pieces of jewelry he had made for Susan Sarandon. He remembered the price of everything and recalled Gore as a formidable businessman.

Toward the end of his time in Ravello, Gore had dispatched Muzius Dietzmann to Giorgio with a kilo bar of what he believed to be solid gold. Giorgio's impression was that this had been a literary prize or perhaps payment for royalties blocked in some country. The details were sketchy except for Gore's desire to sell the gold bar before he moved to the States and his belief that it should command a price of thirty thousand euros.

Giorgio smiled ruefully. "I examined it and noticed some markings. They indicated it wasn't pure gold. Far from it."

He didn't know whether Gore had gotten shortchanged or cheated outright. But he had no choice but to tell Muzius to tell Signor Vidal that the bar was worth no more than three thousand euros.

"I'm sure he wasn't happy," I said.

"I don't know. He said nothing about that to me. He was always a gentleman, a *grande uomo*. He didn't argue. He accepted what I offered."

When I mentioned that Gore's will had left all his money to Harvard University and nothing, not even the house in California, to his family, Giorgio shrugged his hunched shoulders and said, "When you promise to give somebody something, the time to do it is when you're alive. Once you're dead . . ." He shrugged again.

Then, with no change in tone of voice, he continued, "There were two donkeys climbing a mountain. One was fast and frisky. The other soon tired and asked, 'Why are you hurrying?' The first donkey said, 'I'm not tired, because I'm carrying gold.' He easily beat his friend to the mountaintop. The slow donkey had a long time to consider what he had heard, and when he reached the summit, he said, 'You got here first, but remember, we're both still asses.'"

Sitting amid trays of precious stones and gold, Giorgio added, "Sometimes men forget that. Not just Signor Vidal. Many people."

Heading back to Rome, I remembered an exchange between Vidal and Norman Mailer that Gore had reported in a letter to Muriel Spark. The two old warriors had been lamenting their reduced circumstances when Mailer observed by way of consolation, "'At least, Gore, in the future, you and I will be cults.' My cold response: 'A cult may be good enough for you, but I expected to be a major religion.'"

Another great line, but one that when the laughter died revealed the fault that ran through Gore's reasoning. Whatever he got in life, he expected, no, he demanded, more. But in the end it struck me that although his ravenous ambition had often been frustrated, it was no bad thing that rather than becoming president or a Nobel Prize winner or the darling of academics, Gore Vidal remains in the memory, incised on the walls and recalled in the legends of a millennially ancient village that he himself regarded as the most beautiful spot on earth.

Acknowledgments

Like many of my books, *Sympathy for the Devil* took shape over decades, slowly accreting cells like a coral reef. During Gore Vidal's lifetime, I often wrote articles about him for publications as varied as *The London Magazine, House & Garden, Architectural Digest, European Travel & Life*, and *The Independent*. Then after his death I did a reminiscence for *The Washington Post*, which prompted a number of people to urge me to do a memoir about our friendship. Jason Berry may have been the first to encourage me, and I owe him a debt of appreciation.

My thanks also to my agent, Michael Carlisle, who was immediately enthusiastic and guided me through a long proposal and outline—to which Jonathan Galassi, much to my gratitude, offered a contract.

But my greatest debt is to friends in Rome—to Donald and Luisa Stewart for their recollections of Gore and for their photographs; to Lucy Clink and Jeremy Cherfas, who read an early draft of the manuscript and accompanied me on the final trip to Ravello; to Joan Geller, who provided snapshots and anecdotes; to Christina Nagorski for her photographs; to Desmond O'Grady, longtime friend and tennis partner; to Dr. Susan Levenstein for keeping me healthy over the years in Italy; to Dana Prescott, a constant creative presence, and her husband, Donald Carroll, whose legal acumen has thus far kept me out of an Italian jail.

My son Marc read what I believed to be the final draft of *Sympathy for the Devil* and kindly pointed out how I could improve it. My son Sean, his wife, Desi, and our granddaughter, Arden, all took time from their movie careers to support Papabear.

As always, I confess that nothing would have been possible without Linda, whose love and encouragement, patience and understanding, not to mention her typing, have sustained me through forty-seven years and twenty books.